ISSUES IN MORAL AN̲ ON

Editor: Mike Bottery

ASPECTS OF EDUCATION
JOURNAL OF THE
INSTITUTE OF EDUCATION
THE UNIVERSITY OF HULL

NUMBER THIRTY SEVEN
1987

First Published 1987

© THE UNIVERSITY OF HULL 1987

ISBN 0-85958-223-X

Opinions expressed are entirely those
of the contributors concerned.

Aspects of Education is published
by the University of Hull
Institute of Education and printed
by the University of Hull

CONTENTS

EDITORIAL INTRODUCTION

The mention of Moral and Values Education can cause at least two kinds of adverse reaction from the non-professional. One is the slightly raised eyebrows, the "Oh yes", and the swift move to how Liverpool are going to win the championship yet again. Moral Education, it is sometimes assumed, is about how children are taught to be good, and a Moral and Values Educator, it is believed, is a specialist in certain forms of indoctrination.

The other reaction is one, again from the uninitiated, where a one-line definition is being sought. Forget the protestations of the academics, it is said: everyone did History, Geography and English Literature at school, so it's clear what they're about. History is the study of the past, Geography is the study of different places, English Literature is the study of novels and poetry. But Moral Education? What's that?

H. L. Mencken once said that to every complex problem there existed a solution which was neat, simple and wrong. And a neat, simple answer is being demanded here.

The options, then, seem to be either: say nothing, and leave the observer with false impressions and hence do the subject an injustice; provide the observer with a one-liner and again do the subject an injustice; or serve up a five-course meal to someone who doesn't seem particularly hungry.

Moral and Values Education is about Morals and Values, but it is also about Education. And by this is meant Education as opposed to Instruction. It is, I would argue, more about a process than about a product. It is about the pupil's journey to self-knowledge, about possible relationships with other people and things. It is necessarily a personal journey. This is not to say that there are no similarities between journeys. All involve personal growth, the development of self-concept and self-esteem, the increasing ability to empathise to others. All are concerned with respect for persons, with fairness and justice, with truthfulness, with keeping promises and contracts. And all must draw attention to the effects of society upon the individual, to the responsibilities to the world we live in, and to the other creatures who share it with us.

The subject *is* difficult to understand or describe, and that is because it is in many ways too close to us, and there is so much of it. And perhaps the really sad thing is that in an age when people want neat simple definitions and solutions to problems, the conscientious educator wants to do just the opposite – he or she wants to stress their complexity. Little wonder, then, that the Moral and Values Educator may have difficulty deciding how to answer a seemingly simple question.

The readings in this book do not attempt the impossible. They do not

1

attempt neat, simple definitions, and follow that with justifications for these neat and simple definitions. What they do is to present the reader with a wide-ranging selection of interests in the area, tied together by a loose common thread. In so doing, they aim to do three things. Firstly, by their diversity they give some idea of the complexity and fascination of the area. Secondly, both in spite of, and because of, this diversity, they tend to throw up similar questions and issues from different angles. And lastly, they suggest and point to other related areas of enquiry.

The reader will certainly want some kind of overview of the area in order to find his bearings. Mike Cross' article leads into the area in a very practical way. Anyone who knows Mike will know that he is passionate in bringing Moral Education out of academic ivory towers and into the world of the practitioners. His article takes the view that neither absolutism nor relativism is necessary or advisable in this area. Moral Education must be about the individual's progress through reflection and realisation of values within a rational framework. This involves a clear structure for curricular involvement rather than a 'we do it all the time' reply, and gives teachers clear guidance in their role as clarifier and facilitator in the process, rather than as an inculator of values. This process, it is argued, must also be reflected in the workings of the schools as a community, for all too often the school as an institution can work in opposition to the school's expressed aims and curricula.

Patrick Costello's article highlights a dilemma brought out in the previous article – the dilemma of obedience and autonomy in moral education. It does so whilst focussing on one particular, but immensely important concept within the moral domain, that of indoctrination. Patrick reviews the literature in the field, and presents his own interpretation of what is meant by the term, cleansed of normal pejorative overtones. In doing so, he takes a very practical view of what can and should be achieved, and argues that in the early years, indoctrination may be unavoidable, whilst in later years, there may be occasions when indoctrination may be desirable. The strength of Patrick's article rests both in its academic rigour, and in the commonsense approach it takes. It provides a stimulating counterweight to more excessive pleas for child autonomy.

At first glance, the stand may seem to be diametrically opposed to that of Mike Cross, and to the following article by Mike Bottery. However, all of these writers approach the question of obedience and autonomy from different angles, and it is well to note that whilst they tend to give different emphases to their answers, there are still similarities in their conclusions.

Where Patrick Costello argues for the intervention of authority in the early years, this in most cases being diminished as the child gets older, the next article by Mike Bottery argues *downwards* towards early years of development from ages where authority is not seen as having the major

2

role in moral education. These two articles can therefore be seen as attacking the same sorts of problems from different angles. The latter article argues that the topics of moral and values education and child rights are conceptually linked, and that an appreciation of the extent of children's rights provides a justification for moral and values education. In support of its argument, it considers both psychological and historical evidence, and suggests that children's abilities are almost certainly under-estimated, and children are therefore not granted rights to which they are entitled. If the article leans towards the freedom and autonomy of the child, it does not necessarily argue against arguments from authority, but rather asks for the proper consideration of both sides. At the very least, it hopefully will stimulate those who support other positions to take psychological and historical evidence into consideration when formulating their own approach.

So far, then, various issues have been considered with that of authority and autonomy being particularly prominent. But there is another kind of approach in this area, which can be seen as Pastoral Care when translated into organisational terms within the school. Paula Stott's article continues then, with an overview of the variety of possible approaches to Pastoral Care in schools. Her article shows that Pastoral Care at the present time lacks clear definition, and in fact tends to be an umbrella term for a variety of needs – the school's as an institution, the teacher's as a prop with disruptive pupils, the children's as an adjunct to an academic orientation, and as a central aim of the school in the development of 'whole child'. Paula argues that if Pastoral Care is seen primarily as a system for helping the child, one must ask the question of whether it really helps towards the development of autonomy, or the development of an acceptance of the status quo. Once again, but this time at the organisational level, the dilemma of autonomy and obedience raises its head.

This concern with the structural implementation of Pastoral Care in schools is followed by an article from practitioners within the field of values education itself. Anyone who has the good fortune to see Humberside Theatre in Education in action will know just how stimulating and thought-provoking their work is. The article is concerned with using Drama to involve children in feeling, thinking about, and discussing the kinds of topics involved in the area of moral and values education. In this article by the company, they describe and justify the approach they take to values education, illustrated by two of the productions they have taken into Humberside schools. Those who have seen them in action will be interested to see how their underlying rationale links in with the issue of authority and autonomy in education. And anyone who has *not* had the opportunity to see them should be sufficiently impressed by the article to want to seek them out.

The final article in the collection by Derek Webster tackles a number of difficult and important questions in a witty and learned manner. In many people's minds, the issue of authority and autonomy in values education is brought most clearly into focus when discussing its connection with Religious Education. This is one of the problems Derek raises in a tour through questions asked of the theologian by the philosopher, the religious person by the secular enquirer. Initially dealing with such questions as the notion of religion being no more than a picturesque way of living morally, with the status of 'God' and 'Good', the perils of the Naturalistic Fallacy, and the obscurity of esoteric terminology, he then tackles the problems of rationality and authority in matters religious and moral, and locates the essential stand as one of self-discovery via reasoning, experience, and the discovery of Natural Law. As with other articles in the volume, it gives clear answers without seeing them as necessarily being of the either/or variety. It also is an excellent way to complete this series of articles, for it points beyond morality per se, implicitly asking the question 'why be moral?'

Whilst the issue of authority and autonomy has assumed a major role in this volume, nevertheless there is both a recurrence of certain other themes, and an enrichment of concepts mentioned briefly by one writer which are given more detailed analysis by others. This can only be for the good of the subject as a whole. If the reader comes away from reading this collection with an interest in the area, and an appreciation of its importance and complexity, then I think that this edition of 'Aspects' will have done its job.

Mike Bottery

THE NEVER ENDING STORY: MORAL VALUING AS AN IMPORTANT APPROACH TO MORAL EDUCATION

Mike Cross

"If one believes in nothing, if nothing makes sense, if we can assert no value whatever, everything is permissible and nothing important. There is no pro or con; the murderer is neither right nor wrong. One is free to stoke the crematory fires, or to give one's life to the care of lepers. Wickedness and virtue are just accident or whim".

Albert Camus "The Rebel"

"I thought that moral education was something that you either did or didn't do"

Primary School Teacher, Salford

Valuing is central to all conscious behaviour involving judgements, choices and decisions. Yet whilst everyone judges, chooses and decides pretty well automatically or at least as a matter of course there is no reason to suppose that everyone will inevitably or necessarily perform these functions well on all occasions or even on any. Indeed experience suggests that for at least part of the time the reverse is true. Nowhere is this more evident than when considering behaviour in the area of moral judging, choosing and deciding. In that area, in which all of us who are actually conscious are participants, the capacity to clarify the values of oneself and of others is crucial. Only thus can it be said with any degree of certainty that a particular judgement, choice or decision is one that can be classified as belonging to the moral area. So many avowedly "moral" decisions fail to reflect moral values at all. This essay, as opposed to a closely argued thesis, attempts to take such observations seriously and thus proposes an approach to the moral development of all children.

The starting point is that moral education cannot be completely ignored or deliberately avoided by schools. Something must be going on simply by virtue of being with other people in an institutional setting which has its own sets of norms and expectations. And not simply "being" but developing in that institution. It should be noted that this raises issues to do with the obligations that schools have towards society and of course the obligations that society has towards schools. Whilst the full nature and range of those obligations cannot be examined here one particular point must be made. Although "something must be going on" it is by no means enough to be satisfied with that as an approach. The obligations of both the school and society demand that what the "something" is must be understood.

⎰Moral Education is a practical subject. Ultimately it is about what people do and, by extension, who they are. Most people would agree that children should learn to act morally. Yet what that actually means is unlikely to meet with universal agreement. Part of the problem is the widespread belief that moral absolutes do not exist. After all, it's all a matter of opinion, isn't it? It is understandable therefore, that the fear of imposing morality and even indoctrination should be uppermost in the minds of many teachers.⎱In fact the situation is quite invidious. One is likely to be damned if one imposes moral values and one is likely to be damned if one doesn't. Cultural diversity is a mixed blessing. In order to accommodate cultural diversity it is tempting to embrace moral relativism. However, that would be a mistake. Moral relativism is more than the descriptive claim that individuals or cultures frequently accord different priorities to particular values or indeed adhere to different values altogether. Moral relativism is the prescriptive view that all values, including moral values, should be considered equally valid when making judgements or deciding upon a course of action. Consequently any judgement or course of action is no better or worse than any other. However, in accepting that, the whole point of morality is lost. It is perfectly possible for conflicting ethical principles to be equally valid but their validity must be established on moral grounds. The conflict may remain but that is the nature of moral valuing, judging and acting.

Diversity of values is one way of defining the identity of different individuals and communities. The investigation of such diversity as an aim of education does not however excuse relativism. A number of responses are possible. First, there is probably far more agreement between different groups within society than is generally realised. Fairness, consideration for others, loyalty and honesty would surely feature among a list of shared values since without that bare minimum it is hard to understand how any society could survive. What those values mean in terms of behaviour might well vary and so might the priority that each was accorded in any specific situation. Nevertheless, potentially at least, some common ground exists. Second, it is possible to agree on what moral valuing as a process involves irrespective of which moral values become ultimately significant for the individual. Thus the process of moral valuing can be distinguished from the process of, say, aesthetic valuing. This suggests that certain valuing capacities can be developed and furthermore that children can be given the experience of participating in the valuing process on something other than an ad hoc basis. Encountering a variety of perspectives is an important aspect of the child's moral growth. That kind of enrichment should not lead simply to a supermarket type of selection of

6

values. Questions of what an individual's moral values might be are not answered simply by picking a pre-packed assortment but by individuals engaging in the process of valuing.

Placing the word "moral" in front of "value" or "decision" indicates that it is a value or a decision of a particular type. It is one thing to argue that, "It is unattractive to see people starving in the streets" and quite another to argue that "it is wrong that people should be starving in the streets when there is enough food in the world for everyone." One argument invokes aesthetic values and the other invokes moral values. Of course, both arguments might be correct. Yet their respective implications for behaviour can be startlingly different. In one case a course of action might be to clean up the streets and in the other an appropriate response might be to investigate the means by which food surpluses could be equitably distributed. It is important, therefore, to be clear about the process involved. The checklist that follows (Figure 1) is not meant to indicate discrete activities. An individual can be engaged in some or all of these activities at the same time. The activities that are part of the process of moral valuing have been separated in order to provide some clarity about educational goals. They indicate the kinds of activities in which to engage children and the kinds of competencies to be fostered if children are to make moral value decisions for themselves. Both the explicit valuing processes and the complementary processes make assumptions about what are educationally desirable activities.

Interestingly a number of schools programmes espouse the complementary processes without indicating their value implications. The intention here is to provide an overview of associated activites which might promote the moral development of the child.

There is the truly awful, "We do this all the time anyway" syndrome. True, values decisions are constantly being made in schools and that will inevitably have an effect on young people. Everything from individual classroom management and lesson planning to curriculum policy and school organisation involves value judgements. However, as has already

7

Figure 1.

The Process of Moral Valuing	
Explicit Valuing Processes	**Complementary Processes**
Identifying and clarifying the issue Understanding the nature of the problem and the possible principles and values involved. Identifying worthwhile ends in terms of traits of character, ideals, actions. Awareness of relevant social norms, expectations and prevailing values and beliefs.	Both standards of judgement and awareness of feelings are involved. A degree of rationality (consistency and generality) is required as is the ability to compare and contrast. Awareness of feelings is an aspect of understanding the meaning of a value e.g. how honesty and dishonesty, respectively, feel.
Gathering and using information Knowing what sorts of information to find concerning the relevant facts, where to find it and how to use it.	Gathering, organizing, analyzing and evaluating data. Willingness and ability to ask for guidance.
Identifying alternative courses of action Recognising the existence of different means for achieving the desired/desirable end in the light of prevailing principles and values.	Willingness to accept that there is always an alternative. Recognising the possibility of alternatives whether each or any are actualised or not.
Choosing Choosing from alternatives in the light of possible consequences and with an under-standing of personal motives. Predicting likely outcomes and accepting them. Demonstrating rationally, "Can the choice be applied to new cases?" Prepared to give and ask for justification. Self-awareness and awareness of others. Protecting personal interests and accepting that others have an equal right to the protection of their interests. Achievement planning and the identification of strategies to achieve the goal.	Recognising that not all choices can be of equal worth (if they are then why bother to make them?) Capacity for imaginative and creative responses. Self-evaluation, Role-taking: understanding the others' point of view, beliefs and feelings. Communicating; sending and receiving clear messages about needs and desires. (Values do not develop in a vacuum but through interaction with others. Sharing can have a clarifying effect in confirming or changing choices).
Acting Judging what, how and when by relating the act to identified principles or values and judging its appropriateness. Identifying the connection between values and action. Acting repeatedly, consistently, skilfully.	Cooperating Managing conflict.

been indicated, it is questionable indeed to claim that such occurences constitute structured educational experiences. Such an approach would certainly not be tolerated in Mathematics or Art or in anything else where it is obvious that there are certain forms of knowledge, concepts and skills to be acquired. It is laughable to suppose that an ability in Art could be developed simply by looking at the way in which the school is decorated. In fact such an approach would be more likely to have an opposite effect and by analogy the same could be true of moral development as well. Consequently, even if moral values are transmitted the children will not necessarily be acquiring the capacity to clarify, defend or develop their own values.

Placing emphasis ultimately on the kind of thing that moral valuing is, rather than on the instilling of particular values, has three important consequences:

* By having the opportunity to engage in the process of valuing children will be helped to understand the implications of particular values and hence organise their own value system. This does not mean that an understanding of existing norms can be ignored. Indeed they could not be. The valuing process is a process about something and by its very nature demands that attention be paid to as wide a range of values as is reasonable.

* Children are able to reflect on particular principles and come to be able to make and act upon value judgements for themselves. They will thus be able to respond to issues as they occur and which could neither be foreseen nor rehearsed.

* The emphasis on the kind of thing that moral valuing is enables the teacher to respond to the notion that there can be no ill-considered moral opinions since the form of moral valuing imposes on those opinions those criteria that are inherent in the nature of moral valuing.

This in turn provides a response to four key questions:

* What criteria should be used to define the nature of morality?

* Who should decide what values should be taught?

* What safeguards are there to prevent indoctrination?

* Is moral valuing caught rather than taught?

The nature of morality can be defined in a variety of ways. Reference may be made to specific virtues or to stages of cognitive development. Appeals to custom, law or scripture may be made. However, in every case certain individuals and groups will dissent. It is more likely that a wider consensus will be achieved over the nature of the valuing process and whilst that process is by no means value free it takes a "step back" from other approaches and can be used as an evaluative tool for those engaged in the task of clarifying their own position. The same applies to the question of "Who should decide what values should be taught?" It is the process of valuing rather than values as such that is taught. That in itself provides a safeguard against indoctrination and whilst this approach accepts that children will "catch" values from a variety of sources (parents, peers, media, etc) it also insists that the process of valuing can be taught in the sense that individuals can come to understand more clearly what it involves and put that understanding into practice.

The main task of the teacher, therefore, is as a clarifier and facilitator of the valuing process. The emphasis here is on the inculcation of valuing competencies rather than on the inculcation of a particular set of values. Children will be encouraged to come to their own decisions. However, a delicate sensitivity is necessary. Questions about worthwhile ends delve into sensitive areas of the individual's life. The proper atmosphere for sharing must be developed. Building a sense of security is essential if children are to be encouraged to think for themselves and develop the confidence to express their own thoughts. Moral values education does not flourish when children feel compelled to conform to the peer group.

The appropriateness of certain styles of learning quickly becomes apparent. At all levels it is clearly the case that the aggressive imposition of personal perspectives, the unequivocal denial of alternative perspectives or simply favouring those of like mind are not procedures which are conducive to the process of moral valuing, or to developing the ability of children to engage in that process. Essentially an aim of moral education must be that children are better able to do something for themselves, namely clarify, defend and act upon their own values. Thus children must become involved in that process and be participants in their own learning and indeed help to promote the learning of each other.

Consequently an experiential approach to learning would appear to have much to recommend it. Competency in moral valuing is actually promoted by asking the children to make the value judgements rather than being talked to about values. There is a crucial distinction here between valuing and learning about values. Both have their place since the former cannot occur without reference to the latter in any complete sense. However, the emphasis is on the former. It is simply the case that people do make choices and act upon them. It would seem reasonable therefore to take steps to ensure that people are able to operate effectively in this area.

The approach that is recommended therefore is one that has certain key characteristics:

10

Personal involvement is an aspect of the process since the entire individual emotionally and cognitively is in the learning event.

The learner is instrumental in making meaning at an individual level and this is built into the learning experience.

The learning is evaluated by the learner since it is the learner who knows whether it is meeting a need or illuminating an area of ignorance, uncertainty or confusion.

Potentially the learning makes a difference to the behaviour, the attitudes and perhaps even the personality of the learner.

The associated ideas whereby the teacher accepts that the children can think and learn for themselves and from each other, that the teacher's task is primarily in fostering the continuing process of learning are in themselves value messages that are part of the moral learning of the child.

At this point two further key questions are raised:–

* What is to be the stance of the teacher both with regard to coping with moral issues in a multi-cultural context and to giving due accord to the range of possible responses to such issues that might be elicited?

* Are there any issues over which it is permissible for the teacher to take a definite stand?

Particular positions could be adopted by the children which might run counter to the claims of certain minority groups or indeed to the expectations of society as a whole. There may be certain issues over which the teacher might wish to make a definite statement. "No Johnny, genocide *is* wrong". For the teacher the balance between saying nothing in order to avoid influencing the children and risking such influence in order to prevent some sort of harm occurring is a matter for personal and professional judgement and may be linked with both the issue at hand and the maturity of the children. However, it must be remembered that the teacher too is part of the group and as such should take part in the valuing process. If nothing else this at least ensures that the process is rigorously pursued and respected.

The rigorous pursuit of the valuing process takes the moral education debate beyond questions of curriculum design and implementation. Important though such questions are the valuing process raises further issues to do with the nature of schooling. In particular the process of moral valuing has implications for the school as a community. Indeed by reflecting on the children's involvement in the valuing process it is possible to question whether schools in general are communities at all. Are they places where young people develop a sense of community? Do the young people

11

really know each other, really care about each other or really have a sense of belonging? To what extent are young people involved in sharing the responsibility for making the decisions about their own behaviour, their classes and the school as a whole?

⌐By illuminating questions about the child's involvement in the valuing process at a practical level moral education unearths the moral nature of the school. The ways in which moral values are expressed in the day-to-day practices of the school quickly come under scrutiny. In a sense moral education is not to be found in ready-made packages but in school structures where real things actually happen to real people. This may be a daunting prospect. In fact it is much healthier than the usual reliance on curriculum projects of one sort or another many if not the majority of which have had little long-term impact on the ways in which schools operate regardless of the importance of such projects in terms of educational theory. The truth is that schools are more than syllabi, course requirements and instructional materials. There is a case for saying that the school viewed as a community containing the features just indicated runs counter to the school viewed as an institution. There is a need for arrangements that might promote dialogue, participation and fellowship whilst at the same time meeting institutional purposes. What is clear is that as part of the valuing process young people must be provided with the opportunity to act on their values. The "community" of the school is one of the contexts in which that will occur. Attention should be paid to the ways in which people relate to each other and take responsibility for their own learning and behaviour.⌐

⌐ The process of moral valuing in itself assumes certain value positions. Assumptions are being made about the nature of humanity, morality and education. People are dynamic rather than passive and they are responsible and accountable. Certain precepts and principles may be generally accepted yet their application can be a matter for individual choice given particular circumstances. The emphasis on moral valuing endorses this by suggesting that people have to engage in that process for themselves. So it is that value judgements are implicit in the description of the valuing process.⌐ Rationality and reasoning indicate the value of critical analysis. Choice indicates the value of creativity, imagination and self-determination. Other values may also be apparent as the valuing process is examined. The justification that endorses those values resides in educational grounds.

A specific example may serve as an illustration. The view of moral development that is prevalent in this culture is one where the development is a movement towards autonomy. However, the concept of autonomy can be misleading and in order to be acceptable must be situated in an acceptable educational context. Autonomy might be used as short-hand for "standing on one's own feet" and not being swayed by the opinions of others. This sense of autonomy has something to recommend it except that moral maturity also carries with it the notion that the individual should, when necessary, be willing and able to ask for guidance. It does not imply that such guidance must always be followed. However, the individual who never seeks guidance runs the risk of being both arrogant and in error. If alternatively, autonomy means that individuals can clarify their own values be they Christian, Islamic, Marxist, secular Humanist or whatever, and act accordingly, then there are educational grounds for pursuing that aim for such is the mark of an educated person. The process of valuing is one which promotes autonomy in a way whereby either challenge or commitment is possible.

Values underpin and give importance to both ideals and beliefs yet at the same time values can be distinguished from both. Ideals don't always imply a choice yet values do. The culture in which a child grows up may hold certain ideals but these only become individually held values when a person uses those ideals as a personal way of making choices about something that is held to be appropriate for the individual. Ideals become personally held values as and when they provide direction for personal behaviour. It is the value dimension of an ideal that gives an ideal life. Beliefs on the other hand are to do with things that may be true or not, correct or incorrect. A value is a different sort of judgement which is to do with things being good or bad, desirable or undesirable, worthwhile or not. Values are to do with the appropriateness of things and the degree to which those things matter, not just their existence. Neither is necessarily true of beliefs and cannot be until the valuing process is applied to beliefs. The valuing process is not a substitute for ideals or beliefs but a means for establishing their significance for the individual child. Therein lies its importance.

INDOCTRINATION IN THE CLASSROOM

Patrick Costello

The purpose of this paper is to offer a qualified justification for the use of indoctrination in schools. I shall proceed by examining current conceptions of 'indoctrination' and by arguing for a new conception. Implicit in my analysis will be a rejection of the view which finds widespread acceptance nowadays, namely that 'indoctrination' is necessarily a pejorative term.

Some years ago, Ian Gregory[1] remarked that despite the 'highly embryonic state' in which philosophy of education then found itself, one of the concepts which had received most attention from philosophers of education was 'indoctrination', about which, even at that time, much had been written. Three years earlier, Gregory and Woods[2] had noted the 'voluminous literature' devoted to 'indoctrination' and had expressed doubt that anything new could be said on the subject. Yet, seventeen years later, we find that contributions on the topic (from both within and outside academic circles) are as numerous as ever; indeed discussions of indoctrination are at the present time very much in vogue.

One has only to open a daily newspaper, or a copy of *The Times Educational Supplement,* to reveal headlines such as 'Tories declare war on indoctrination',[3] '"History" course is bunk, say teachers',[4] '"Political danger in our schools"',[5] 'Schools rapped in "politics row"',[6] 'Warning on propaganda posing as peace studies',[7] 'World Studies "propaganda" – Scruton',[8] etc. This latter article refers to a pamphlet by Roger Scruton,[9] professor of aesthetics at Birkbeck College, London, in which he argues that World Studies teaching is indoctrinatory rather than educational. A second pamphlet, of which Scruton is co-author, makes a similar attack on Peace Studies, and takes a passing swipe at 'Women's Studies', 'Black Studies', 'Gay Studies', and 'Sports Studies'.[10] A third pamphlet, again co-written by Scruton, offers a Draft Amendment to the 1944 Education Act, which recommends stern action to be taken against those teachers who seek to indoctrinate their pupils.[11]

Now it should not be thought that misgivings about indoctrination have been expressed only by right-wing politicians and university lecturers. Teachers and pupils alike have added their voices to the protest. Ray Honeyford, former Headmaster of Drummond Middle School in Bradford, in a newspaper article entitled 'The Blackboard Bungle', writes that 'an increasing number of teachers are not prepared to distinguish between education and indoctrination.'[12] More recently, an article called 'Lessons in a New Class Struggle',[13] gives details of a newly-formed group called 'CHOIS' (Children Opposed to Indoctrination in Schools), whose founder, Myfanwy Robson, is only fourteen years old.

We must now ask whether the numerous accounts of 'indoctrination' which have been offered over the years by philosophers of education have contributed anything to the above discussions. A charitable answer to this question is 'very little'. Indeed it seems to me that many suggested conceptions have succeeded only in blurring vital distinctions, an appreciation of which would lead to a long overdue reappraisal of the term.

Gatchel[14] has argued that viewing 'indoctrination' with opprobrium is a comparatively recent development in the world of education. Historically the term simply meant 'teaching doctrines', and was not looked upon as what philosophers call a 'boo' word, i.e., something to be given a negative value. Nowadays, however, 'indoctrination' is seen as a term to be compared unfavourably with, for example, 'education', which is seen as having positive value in itself. Thus, while 'indoctrination' is thought to be the concern of Communists,[15] Roman Catholics,[16] pacificists,[17] and certain other proponents of political education,[18] 'educating' is said to be what we 'good' teachers are engaged in.

This myopic view of indoctrination is safeguarded, to some extent, by the arguments of philosophers who assert that 'indoctrination' is a matter of the methods used by the teacher, or the subject matter he conveys to his students, or his intention to indoctrinate. Various combinations of these features have also been suggested as providing the 'essence' of the term. A fourth alternative, which views 'indoctrination' in terms of the *outcome* of a teaching transaction, has been ignored by many authors, and where it is mentioned, it is often treated briefly and summarily rejected. I shall argue that this notion is central to the concept.

In some recent educational writings, a disturbing trend has become evident. The term 'indoctrination' is used to refer to the inculcation of those values with which the writer disagrees, while 'education' is said to involve inducting into values of which he approves. A good example of this tendency can be found in *Educational and Indoctrination*, in which the authors suggest that there are five elements which constitute 'indoctrination':

(1) Conclusions are foregone . . .
(2) The conclusions form part of a constellation, whose meaning is to be found in a 'hidden unity', based (on an) emotional or political attitude.
(3) The conclusions are premises to action, and form the fundamental starting-point of a political 'programme'.
(4) The conclusions are part of a closed system of mutually confirming dogma, which serves to consolidate and validate the emotional unity from which it springs.

15

(5) They are typically established not by open discussion, but by closing the mind to alternative viewpoints, and perhaps even by vilifying or denouncing opposition.[19]

An examination of the pamphlet reveals that the term 'indoctrination' has been used to denote those values which Scruton et al. do not wish to see introduced into educational institutions. However, it is significant that religious education, which has traditionally been viewed as a paradigm case of indoctrination,[20] is not included for censure. Indeed we are told that religion forms 'an ineliminable part of our constitution as rational beings'.[21] It should also be noted that the authors themselves, while arguing for values which they believe to be the very antithesis of 'indoctrination', employ the five criteria which they suggest are central to the term.

One thing is clear from this brief explication. We need to do more than to use the term 'indoctrination' simply to indicate those values which we do not share, if it is to function meaningfully within the realm of educational discourse. We must have a criterion which we are able to apply without fear or favour to *All* values. In what follows, I shall attempt to provide such a criterion.

In looking for a plausible characteristic (or set of characteristics) in terms of which 'indoctrination' might be defined, philosophers of education have sought a set of necessary and sufficient conditions for applying the concept. Those who have posited a particular content as being central to the term, have pinned their arguments on a supposed conceptual link between 'indoctrination' and 'doctrines'.[22] This approach has been summed up in Antony Flew's bold statement, 'No doctrines, no indoctrination!'[23] However, Flew's claim cannot be sustained, since it has been argued convincingly that (1) there is merely a casual connection between 'indoctrination' and 'doctrines', (2) it is possible to indoctrinate not only doctrines but also true and false propositions.[24] In short, content of a doctrinal nature is not a necessary condition of 'indoctrination'.

Let us now turn our attention to another criterion which, it is argued, is constitutive of 'indoctrination', namely intention. A number of philosophers have given support to the view that for indoctrination to be taking place, for example in a classroom, the teacher must *intend* to indoctrinate.[25] On this argument, unintentional indoctrination is ruled out by definition. To rebut such an inference, we may invoke a well-worn but effective epigram: 'The road to indoctrination is paved with good (as well as bad) intentions.' This, I believe, precisely locates the major weakness in arguments supporting the 'intention' thesis, since it is possible for teachers to indoctrinate their pupils *unintentionally*.[26]

For example, Cooper[27] argues that unintentional indoctrination may be engaged in by indoctrinators whom he terms 'sincere'. A 'sincere' indoctrinator is defined as 'one who himself believes the propositions he is

16

teaching, and who thinks it important that his students should believe them precisely because, according to him they are true'.[28] While it should be noted that it is not only 'sincere' indoctrinators (as defined by Cooper) who can unintentionally indoctrinate,[29] the existence of such a group poses a problem for Ivan Snook, a leading proponent of the 'intention' criterion. Snook argues, on the one hand, for a 'strong' sense of 'intention', so that someone is indoctrinating if 'in his teaching he is actively desiring that the pupils believe what he is teaching regardless of the evidence'.[30] However, this can be criticized because a sincere indoctrinator, believing the propositions he teaches to be true, and not being aware of any evidence which he would consider as sufficient to count against them, therefore cannot intend for his students to believe such propositions 're-gardless of the evidence'. Indeed, he might well state that, were satisfac-tory evidence to be provided against a proposition p, he would not wish his students to believe that p is true.[31]

Snook[32] also offers a 'weak' sense of 'intention' so that a person is indoctrinating if he foresees it as 'likely or inevitable' that, as a result of his teaching, his pupils will believe what he teaches regardless of the evidence. This attempt to expand the meaning of 'intention' has also been shown to be unsatisfactory, and its demise brings with it the collapse of the 'intention' criterion.[33] Since convincing arguments can be adduced to support the view that one can indoctrinate unintentionally, we must con-clude that attempts to establish 'intention' as a necessary condition of 'indoctrination' have been unsuccessful.

Several writers have argued that 'method' is essential to an understand-ing of 'indoctrination'.[34] On this view, whether a teacher is engaged in indoctrinating his pupils depends on *how* he teaches them. Thomas Benson[35] has argued that there are two main forms of indoctrinatory method: the persuasive presentation and the engineering of assent. Each form has two sub-categories. The biased argument and the dogmatic pre-sentation are illustrative of the persuasive presentation, while depriva-tion of the ability and of the opportunity to withhold assent from a proposition, belong to the engineering of assent. Patricia Smart suggests that 'to talk of indoctrination is to suggest that the teacher uses unfair means to induce the child to come to conclusions which he himself intends to make, but which the subject matter does not necessarily demand.'[36] Finally, according to Hepburn, 'to be indoctrinated is to be prompted non-rationally to a belief or attitude or other state of mind: without, that is, being given or encouraged to seek good grounds.'[37]

We must now ask: (1) Is 'method' a necessary condition of 'indoctrina-tion'? (2) Is 'method' a sufficient condition of 'indoctrination'? In one sense the answer to the first question is 'no' since, as I shall argue pre-sently, a child may become indoctrinated by *rational* methods. Indoctri-natory (i.e. non-rational) methods are, however, both necessary and justifiable in early childhood education. Now if my analysis of 'indoctrination' is acceptable, it will become clear that such methods are not a *sufficient* condition of 'indoctrination'. To see that this is so, we need do no more than to imagine a young child with whom we have employed indoctrinatory methods, but who remains uninfluenced by them, and who therefore does not end up in an indoctrinated state of mind.

The idea that it is necessary to use indoctrinatory methods with young children is one which many writers are unwilling (or unable) to accept. However, the arguments which they offer against this thesis are unconvincing. The tactic usually adopted is to suggest that no part of early childhood education can be called indoctrination if the teacher *intends* that the child will be able to reflect critically, at a later time, on the beliefs into which he has been inducted.[39] 'Intention' has already been shown to be inadequate as a criterion of 'indoctrination'. Brenda Cohen is correct when she asserts that 'if Snook is right and these methods are in fact necessary where very young children are concerned . . . then it may be preferable to concede that there is an area where indoctrination is acceptable.'[40]

In examining a fourth criterion of 'indoctrination', I propose to concentrate on two articles by Paul O'Leary.[41] He is concerned to remedy a deficiency in previously written work on 'indoctrination', namely a tendency to concentrate on analysing statements such as 'X is indoctrinating Y' rather than 'Y is indoctrinated'. He offers two descriptions of the indoctrinated state of mind, both of which, I shall argue, while contributing something to an adequate understanding of 'indoctrination', are ultimately unsatisfactory.

O'Leary begins his first article by suggesting that according to Ivan Snook, there appear to be three general conditions which conjointly are necessary and sufficient to claim that someone is indoctrinated. These are: (1) the belief condition – the indoctrinated person believes a proposition or set of propositions; (2) the epistemic condition – the indoctrinated person believes a proposition or set of propositions 'regardless of the evidence'; (3) the causal condition – the belief condition and the epistemic condition have been brought about because of certain teaching activities.[42]

O'Leary reformulates the belief condition to include to notion of 'doubting that p', and includes a dispositional condition, so that his first description of the indoctrinated state of mind is as follows: 'S believes that p or doubts that p regardless of the evidence and is disposed to reject any q which is offered as a counter-instance to believing that p or doubting that p.'[43] By 1982, O'Leary's definition has undergone certain important changes. His second formulation is: 'Because of T's teaching, S believes that p, regardless of the evidence; and is disposed to reject any q that is offered as a counter-instance to believing that p.'[44]

The following points should be noted: (1) the notion of 'doubting that p' has been left out in the second definition; (2) O'Leary offers a causal condition which is absent in his earlier article. As far as the belief condition is concerned, I can see no reason to reject O'Leary's earlier view that belief and doubt are disjunctively necessary for an adequate understanding of the indoctrinated state of mind. O'Leary himself offers us no reasons as to why he has decided to dispense with the notion of 'doubting that p'. It would seem that just as a teacher may teach for unquestionable belief, so too may he teach for unquestionable doubt. On the traditional view of indoctrination, a teacher can only be accused of indoctrinating if he wishes his pupils to *believe* something unshakably. This would surely allow a teacher who is concerned only to *discredit* certain views, while perhaps offering nothing in their place, to escape the charge of unjustifiable indoctrination.[45] He teaches for unquestionable doubt, not for unquestionable belief. So widening the belief condition to include the notion of 'doubting that p' will allow us to bring what this teacher does within the purview of indoctrination, and so within the realm of culpability.

Turning to the epistemic condition, O'Leary argues that the phrase 'regardless of the evidence' can be interpreted in two ways, since a person can believe or doubt a proposition *without* evidence, or *despite* the evidence.[46] Now while it is no doubt the case that indoctrinated people often believe propositions without or despite the evidence, this is surely not a *necessary* condition of their being in an indoctrinated state of mind. If I teach a child to believe that $2 \times 2 = 4$ in such a way that he rejects all counter-instances to believing it, does this necessarily imply that he believes it *without* evidence?

Certainly it may be the case that the child has come to believe it as a result of learning it by rote, and so has no evidence for it. But, equally plausibly, he may have to come to believe it as a result of a practical demonstration using four cubes. Similarly with a whole host of propositions from all academic subjects. A child may be indoctrinated with regard to a proposition although he has come to believe it or not without evidence, or despite the evidence, but simply *because of* the evidence.

As we have seen, O'Leary's causal condition features only in his second formulation of the indoctrination state of mind. The inclusion of such a condition is considered necessary in order to distinguish between a person who holds views in a fixed way because of someone's teaching, and a person who exhibits a similar tendency due to having been in a motor accident,[47] or because of stupidity or an unwillingness to think for himself.[48] Yet even if we agree with Degenhardt that 'indoctrination does have to be the result of human agency or action',[49] it still seems to be the case that O'Leary's casual condition ('Because of T's teaching') is too limiting.

To begin with, it is not always the case that a charge of indoctrination

19

can be levelled at a *particular* teacher. As Nancy Glock suggests, '"indoctrination" need not apply only to the . . . actions of individuals. It can refer . . . to such policies and practices of *institutions* as do tend to produce indoctrinatory outcomes.'[50]

If the central aim of a certain school is to produce religious conviction in its pupils, it may be impossible to attribute a child's indoctrinated state of mind to an individual teacher. Rather, it is more likely that the school's ethos is responsible for producing a child who responds in a certain way to the inculation of religious beliefs. Mr Smith or Miss Jones may do very little as individuals to promote such beliefs, and yet children may become indoctrinated as a result of a particular lesson given by them. Such indoctrination may have very little to do with the lesson itself – it is possible that teaching received from previous teachers, or at school assemblies, etc., may have contributed substantially to the formulation of fixed religious beliefs.

Similarly, outside agencies such as parents, friends, television, and newspapers, may all combine to produce a child who is 'ripe' for indoctrination. It may therefore be unjust (as well as misleading) to accuse a particular teacher of unjustifiable indoctrination, simply because some of the children in his class end up in an indoctrinated state of mind as a result of a particular lesson. As William Hare notes, 'We cannot, of course, *infer* from the fact that pupils emerge from school with closed minds that their teachers failed to teach in an open-minded way. There may be many forces at work in the homes of students, and in society at large, which make the open-minded attitudes of teachers ineffective.'[51]

However, this is not to suggest that those outside influences which exert themselves on the child may always serve to exculpate a teacher accused of unjustifiably indoctrinating his class. Such a teacher cannot refute the charge simply by reminding us that children are subject to such influences, and by maintaining that it is these influences, and not his teaching, which have led to their developing an indoctrinated state of mind. To determine whether or not the teacher in question has indoctrinated his pupils unjustifiably, we need to (1) determine whether his pupils are in fact indoctrinated, (2) examine his conduct during the lesson(s) in question. It is at this point that content, method and intention are likely to provide us with vital clues in our enquiry. We need to ask whether the teacher's input into the lesson is of the sort which tends to lead to indoctrinatory outcomes.[52] We also need to examine the ethos of the school itself, and such external factors as have already been mentioned. Everything will depend on the particular circumstances of the case. It is on the basis of these considerations, taken together, that we can make a judgement about the teacher's culpability.

To ascertain whether or not indoctrination has taken place during a particular lesson or series of lessons and, if so, what (if anything) it is about those lessons which was indoctrinatory, is by no means easy, and it is not my intention in this paper to examine the issue in any depth. Rather, I am concerned to argue that to attribute a child's indoctrinated state of mind to a particular teacher, as O'Leary does, is not always justifiable. It is of little use to achieve simplicity at the expense of cogency. I propose, therefore, to adopt a modified causal condition, which is 'due to the teaching or influence of Y'. This has the advantage of attributing indoctrination to factors outside a particular classroom, and therefore outside the control of a particular teacher. 'Y' will include institutions, teachers, parents, friends, the media, etc.

O'Leary's first formulation of the dispositional condition is as follows: 'S . . . is disposed to reject any q which is offered as a counter-instance to believing that p or doubting that p'. Now 'q' is ambiguous here, since it is open to two interpretations: (1) a counter-instance which appeals to a present state of affairs or knowledge (for example, 'Paris is the capital of France, not Italy'); (2) a counter-instance which appeals to a putative future state of affairs or knowledge (for example, a possible response to someone who maintains that a Labour government would improve the state of the National Health Service might be: 'But what if a Labour government actually closed down more hospitals than its predecessor?').

Further complications now ensue, since we must ask whether the term 'indoctrinated' can be said to apply to either or both of the following: (1) someone who rejects counter-instances to his believing that p or doubting that p at the time at which they are offered to him, but who later accepts such counter-instances; (2)someone who rejects such counter-instances at the time at which they are offered to him, and at all times in the future.

White[53] maintains that only a person who falls into the latter category can be called 'indoctrinated', since his beliefs are 'unshakable'. However, I wish to argue (along with Callan)[54] that we can call someone 'indoctrinated' even though this state of mind may only be a temporary one. Furthermore, for us to be able to refer to someone as 'indoctrinated', it is only necessary that he rejects any *present* counter-instance at the time at which it is offered to him. It is not necessary that such an individual rejects any putative future counter-instance. For example, let us say that I attempt to indoctrinate a child with a proposition such as 'There are ten rings around the planet Uranus'. In order for me to be able to say that I have succeeded (i.e., that the child has become indoctrinated), it is necessary only that the child rejects the present counter-instances to the proposition (for example, 'Uranus has nine rings around it'). It is not incumbent upon him to reject a putative future counter-instance (for example, 'What if an eleventh ring were to be discovered in 1990?'). This is an important distinction of which O'Leary's analysis fails to take account. Accordingly, 'any q' in his schema must be amended to 'any present q'.

My definition of the 'achievement' aspect of 'indoctrination' can now be stated thus:

> X is indoctrinated with respect to p (a proposition or set of propositions) if, due to the teaching or influence of Y, X believes that p or doubts that p, in such a way that X is disposed to reject any present q which is offered as a counter-instance to believing that p or doubting that p.

Looked at from the point of view of the indoctrinator, the formula becomes:

> Y indoctrinates X with respect to p (a proposition or set of propositions) if Y teaches or influences X to believe that p or doubt that p, in such a way that X is disposed to reject any present q which is offered as a counter-instance to believing that P or doubting that p.

This formulation also implies the achievement of an indoctrinated state of mind. Rather than to suggest that a teacher who failed to bring about such a state of mind in his pupils was engaged in indoctrinating them, it is preferable to say instead that he was *attempting* to indoctrinate them.[55] Or, in cases where we suppose that no intention to indoctrinate is involved on the part of the teacher, we might say that the teaching or influencing of his pupils was such that it *tended towards* an indoctrinatory outcome.[56]

In discussing whether or not being in an indoctrinated state of mind is desirable, O'Leary borrows a phrase from Gilbert Ryle[57] and suggests that when a person is in such a state he is not 'prepared for *variable* calls within certain ranges'. He continues:

> Whether being in a state of mind appropriate to indoctrination is educationally harmful, depends upon (1) whether knowing how to engage in a given activity is thought to be important and (2) whether we construe the activity that students are being taught as subject to variation . . . suppose that knowing how to engage in a given activity is regarded as important, but that the beliefs, skills, and dispositions required for its performance are perfectly suited to all cirmcumstances and not subject to alteration. If we *knew* that a given activity would require no modifications in belief in order to perform it with a minimum degree of competance, then there would be no educational objection to bringing about the state of mind that is characteristic of being indoctrinated.[58]

O'Leary's discussion concentrates on the teaching of *activities* to students. While engaging in such activities necessarily involves the aquisition of certain beliefs, skills, and dispositions. I see no reason why Ryle's passage cannot be used to refer to the teaching of beliefs seen as ends in themselves. Thus it becomes possible to say that when a given belief is not subject to '*variable* calls within certain ranges' (i.e., when there exists, to

22

the best of our knowledge, no warrantable alternative to it), it is justifiable to indoctrinate a child with that belief. The following is a representative sample of beliefs with which children, on this criterion, may justifiably be indoctrinated:

Les Demoiselles d'Avignon was Picasso's first Cubist painting.
The green pigment contained in the leaves of plants is called chlorophyll.
The chemical symbol for copper is Cu.
The balance of visible trade is said to be in surplus if exports exceed imports.
The poem 'Days' was written by Philip Larkin.
In French, 'lundi' means 'Monday'.
Rome is the capital of Italy.
The Lateran Treaty of 1929 established the Vatican City as an independent sovereign state.
All triangles have three sides.
A minim is a musical note that equals to crotchets in time value.
Trotskyism is a form of Communism supporting the views of Leon Trotsy.
The Koran is the sacred book of Islam.
Ohm's Law is expressed in the equation: electromotive force (in volts) = current (in amperes) × resistance (in ohms).

Some comments must be made about the above list. To begin with, it will be noted that the propositions offered cover a wide range of topics. Indeed it is possible to indoctrinate beliefs (as expressed by propositions) in all school subjects, both at primary and secondary level. Secondly, the beliefs to be indoctrinated are all *true* beliefs (i.e., they represent knowledge in various fields). Consequently, such counter-instances as may be offered (expressed as proportions) will be *false*. Thirdly, therefore, these (what I shall category 'A') beliefs do not admit of justifiable alternatives (for example, one would not be warranted in maintaining that some triangles do not have three sides, or that acid will turn red litmus paper blue 'one day'). Category 'A' beliefs represent the state of knowledge as it is (or as we believe it to be) at the time we are engaged in indoctrinating them.

Let us now contrast the above propositions with a list of statements which express value judgements. For example:

Art is imaginative expression.
One should never steal under any circumstances.
The Labour Party offers the most credible alternative to a Conservative government.
The Pope is infallible when he speaks *ex cathedra* to define a doctrine concerning faith or morals.[59]

23

How are these two categories of statement to be distinguished? To begin with, we should say that as regards the latter set of beliefs (which I shall include in category 'B'), it is possible for two people who are both equally well-informed about the nature of aesthetics, morals, politics, and religion, to disagree about them without either party necessarily being regarded as mistaken (or, at least, not mistaken in the sense in which someone who asserted that 'Rome is the capital of France' would be mistaken). In other words, each of the above statements expresses a value judgement to which a warrantable alternative may be offered.[60]

One might therefore suppose that to indoctrinate a child with a belief that expresses a value judgement represents an instance of unjustifiable indoctrination, since the child will be disposed to reject all counter-instances to it, some of which may be equally commendable. In short, he will not be 'prepared for *variable* calls within certain ranges'. With regard to the fields of aesthetics, politics, and religion, I would agree with this argument. In the moral domain, however, the question of whether it is justifiable to indoctrinate beliefs which express value judgements is more complex.

I want to argue that, as far as the child's early moral education is concerned, indoctrinating such beliefs is unavoidable. For example, Derek Wright notes that, according to Piaget, 'the child encounters rules from adults. The source confers a semi-mystical authority upon them; his inability to conceive of other points of view means that once he has accepted the rule into his own thought it cannot be changed or modified'.[61] In other words, a child's early moral development begins by his being inducted into the state of mind which I have characterized as 'indoctrinated'. Furthermore, as O'Hear suggests,

> surely, in all subjects, we begin by simply telling children things. Only later do they come to understand the reasons for what they are told, and to accept or reject things for themselves on their own merits. In morality, as in other areas, there is nothing inconsistent or paradoxical in first laying down things that have to be accepted and later leading pupils to see and evaluate the reasons for what they have been told. Indeed, it is hard to see how reasons could be appreciated for what they are unless they were seen as supporting or justifying propositions that were already understood and (provisionally) accepted.[62]

The moral beliefs with which a child is indoctrinated in his early years come under a third category, which I shall call category 'C' beliefs.

Whether it is justifiable to indoctrinate children with moral beliefs in the later years of their childhood is a difficult question, and one to which I cannot do justice here. Nevertheless, some brief comments are required. It may be that there are certain moral beliefs concerning which we might want older children (and indeed adults) to have closed minds. For example, having attempted to indoctrinate a group of children with a belief such as 'torturing animals is morally wrong', with the result that they accepted the belief, we should not be happy if those children considered that 're-opening the issue (was) a permanent possibility'.[63]

Whether indoctrinating a particular moral belief in this way is warrantable will depend on the arguments which are, or can be, brought forward to support or refute it.[64] These will include considerations such as the non-viability of possible counter-instances to the belief. With regard to beliefs such as 'torturing animals is morally wrong', it may be thought that there are *no* counter-instances which we would wish a child to countenance. Such a belief may therefore be allowed to remain in category 'C', and a teacher can justifiably indoctrinate it. But in the case of a belief such as 'one should never steal under any circumstances', it may be possible (and desirable) to make children aware (at least those who have achieved a certain level of intellectual maturity) that warrantable counter-instances to that belief may be offered. At this point, such a belief no longer belongs in category 'C'. Rather it must be regarded as a category 'B' belief, with which the children referred to above must no longer be indoctrinated.[65]

Casement[66] considers that moral education cannot avoid being indoctrinatory. Faced with this he suggests that we ask a number of questions of any approach to such education. The most important among these are: '"With what beliefs are students indoctrinated?"'[67] Casement acknowledges that 'there will be disagreement about what constitutes a more undesirable case of indoctrination'.[68] However, this 'seems to be something we have to live with. Indoctrination is a complicated matter, and for dealing with it there are no easy answers.'[69]

In conclusion, I suggest that if we see indoctrination in the classroom in terms of the *results* of particular teaching transactions (including reference, where necessary, to the notion of 'influence'), then our perception of 'education' is likely to be altered radically. For now, not only will Communists, Roman Catholics, and pacificists be labelled as 'indoctrinators', but also teachers of mathematics, science, and history. The debate will then shift to the discussion of *which sorts* of indoctrination are acceptable. Much of traditional schooling is indoctrinatory, and we must face up to this. It is a testimony to the 'success' of this schooling that many people believe indoctrination to be exemplified in Communism, or pacificism, but not in their own beliefs.

REFERENCES

1. I. M. M. Gregory, 'Review of *Indoctrination and Education* by I. A. Snook, and *Concepts of Indoctrination: Philosophical Essays* edited by I. A. Snook', *Philosophical Books,* Vol.14, No.2, 1973, pp.25–28.

2. I. M. M. Gregory and R. G. Woods, 'Indoctrination', *Proceedings of the Philosophy of Education Society of Great Britain*, 1970, pp.77–105.
3. *The Times Educational Supplement*, 7 March 1986, p.6.
4. *Daily Express*, 20 September 1985, p.13.
5. *Daily Mail*, 19 March 1985.
6. *Daily Express*, 22 March 1985, p.2.
7. *The Times Educational Supplement*, 29 July 1983, p.8.
8. *The Times Educational Supplement*, 13 December 1985, p.5.
9. R. Scruton, *World Studies: Education or Indoctrination?* Institute for European Defence and Strategic Studies, 1985.
10. C. Cox and R. Scruton, *Peace Studies: A Critical Survey*, Institute for European Defence and Strategic Studies, 1984.
11. R. Scruton, A. Ellis-Jones and D. O'Keeffe, *Education and Indoctrination*, Education Research Centre, 1985.
12. R. Honeyford, 'The blackboard bungle', *Today*, 31 August 1986, pp.10-11.
13. C. Bennett, 'Lessons in a new class struggle', *The Sunday Times*, 2 November 1986, p.44.
14. R. H. Gatchel, 'The evolution of the concept', in I. A. Snook (editor), *Concepts of Indoctrination: Philosophical Essays*, Routledge and Kegan Paul, London, 1972, pp.9-16.
15. F. W. Garforth, *Education and Social Purpose*, Oldbourne, London, 1962; J. Wilson, 'Education and indoctrination', in T. H. B. Hollins (editor), *Aims in Education: The Philosophic Approach*, University Press, Manchester, 1964, pp.24-45.
16. R. M. Hare, 'Adolescents into adults', in T. H. B. Hollins, *op. cit.*, pp.47-70; A. Flew, 'Indoctrination and doctrines', in I. A. Snook (editor), *op. cit.*, pp.67-92; A. Flew, 'Indoctrination and religion', in I. A. Snook (editor), *op. cit.*, pp.106-116.
17. J. Sale, 'Learning how to ask awkward question', *The Guardian*, 28 August 1984, p.9.
18. R. Scruton, A. Ellis-Jones and D. O'Keeffe, *op. cit.*
19. *Ibid.*, pp.25-26.
20. A. Flew, 'Indoctrination and doctrines' and 'Indoctination and religion', in I. A. Snook (editor), *op. cit.*
21. R. Scruton, A. Ellis-Jones and D. O'Keeffe, *op. cit.*, p.45.
22. W. H. Kilpatrick, 'Indoctrination and respect for persons', in I. A. Snook (editor), *op. cit.*, pp.47-54; A. Flew, 'Indoctrination and doctrines', in I. A. Snook (editor), *op. cit.;* Gregory and Woods, *op. cit.*
23. A. Flew, 'Indoctrination and religion', in I. A. Snook (editor), *op, cit.*, p.114.
24. J. P. White, 'Indoctrination without doctrines?', in I. A. Snook

(editor), *op. cit.*, pp.190-201; Elmer J. Thiessen, 'Indoctrination and doctrines', *Journal of Philosophy of Education*, Vol.16, No.1, 1982, pp.3-17; J. Kleinig, *Philosophical Issues in Education*, Croom Helm, London, 1982.

25. R. M. Hare, *op. cit.;* J. P. White, 'Indoctrination and intentions', in I. A. Snook (editor), *op. cit.*, pp.117-130; I. A. Snook, *Indoctrination and Education*, RKP, London, 1972.

26. D. E. Cooper, 'Intentions and indoctrination', *Educational Philosophy and Theory'*, Vol.5, No.1, 1973, pp.43-55; R. Beehler, 'The schools and indoctrination', *Journal of Philosophy of Education*, Vol.19, No.2, 1985, pp.261-272.

27. D. E. Cooper, *ibid.*

28. *Ibid.*, p.44.

29. For example, it seems possible for a teacher with no religious convictions (and who therefore lacks the requisite intention), to indoctrinate his pupils with a belief such as 'Jesus is the Son of God', during a history lessons on the founding of Christianity. Since we should also call such a teacher 'sincere', I propose that the term be understood hereinafter to incorporate examples of this sort.

30. I. A. Snook, *Indoctrination and Education*, p.50.

31. D. E. Cooper, *op. cit.*, p.45. According to P. T. O'Leary ('Indoctrination and the indoctinated state of mind', in D. E. Cochrane and M. Schiralli (editors), *Philosophy of Education: Canadian Perspectives*, Collier Macmillan, Ontario, 1982, p.75), the phrase 'believing regardless of the evidence' can be interpreted in two ways: (1) believing without evidence; (2) believing despite the evidence. When Cooper (p.45) speaks of believing 'in the face of the evidence', he is referring to (2). The 'sincere' indoctrinator would, I suggest, be as unwilling for his students to believe that p is true *without* evidence (here interpreted as 'good reasons') as he would were they to believe that p is true *despite* the evidence.

32. I. A. Snook, *Indoctrination and Education*, p.50.

33. D. E. Cooper, *op. cit.;* J. Kleinig, *op. cit.*

34. R. F. Atkinson, 'Indoctrination and moral education', in I. A. Snook (editor), *op. cit.*, pp.55-66; W. Moore, 'Introduction and democratic method', in I. A. Snook (editor), *op. cit.*, pp93-100; R. Barrow, *Moral Philosophy for Education*, Allen and Unwin, London, 1975; B. G. Mitchell, 'Indoctrination', in *The Fourth R: Durham Report on Religious Education*, Appendix B, S.P.C.K., London, 1970; T. L. Benson, 'The concept of "indoctrination": a philosophical study', Ph.D. thesis, The John Hopkins University, 1975.

35. T. L. Benson, *ibid.*

36. P. Smart, 'The concept of indoctrination' in G. Langford and D. J.

O'Connor (editors), *New Essays in the Philosphy of Education,* RKP, London, 1973, p.37.

37. R. W. Hepburn, 'The arts and the education of feeling and emotion', in R. F. Dearden, P. H. Hirst, and R. S. Peters (editors), *Education and the Development of Reason,* RKP, London, 1972, p.496.

38. B. G. Mitchell, *op. cit.;* W. Moore, *op. cit.;* Paul A. Wagner, Jr., 'Indoctrination and moral education', Ph.D. dissertation, University of Missouri, 1978.

39. R. M. Hare, *op. cit.;* W. H. Kilpatrick, *op. cit.;* K. Thompson, *Education and Philosophy: A Practical Approach,* Blackwell, Oxford, 1972.

40. B. Cohen, *Education and the Individual,* Allen and Unwin, London, 1981, p.51.

41. P. T. O'Leary, 'The indoctrinated state of mind', *Philosophy of Education 1979.* Proceedings of the Philosophy of Education Society, Normal, Illinois, pp.295-303; P. T. O'Leary, 'Indoctrination and the indoctrinated state of mind', in Cochrane and Schiralli, *op. cit.*

42. P. T. O'Leary, 'The indoctrinated state of mind', p.295.

43. *Ibid.,* p.299.

44. P. T. O'Leary, 'Indoctrination and the indoctrinated state of mind', p.77.

45. My aim will be to show that indoctrination is not necessarily indefensible.

46. See reference 31.

47. I. A. Snook, *Indoctrination and Education,* p.40.

48. M. A. B. Degenhardt, 'Indoctrination', in D. I. Lloyd (editor), *Philosophy and the Teacher,* RKP, London, 1976, p.26.

49. *Ibid.*

50. Nancy C. Glock, '"Indoctrination": some pejorative senses and practical proscriptions', Ed.D. dissertation, Harvard University, 1975, p.ii.

51. W. Hare, *Open-mindedness and Education,* McGill-Queen's University Press, Montreal, 1979, p.66.

52. R. Beehler, *op. cit.;* N. Glock, *op. cit.*

53. J. P. White, *op. cit.*

54. E. Callan, 'McLaughlin on parental rights', *Journal of Philosophy of Education,* Vol.19, No.1, 1985, pp,111-118.

55. J. Kleinig, *op. cit.,* p.59.

56. Compare with R. Beehler, *op. cit.,* p. 266.

57. G. Ryle, *The Concept of Mind,* Penguin, Harmondsworth, 1949, p.141.

58. P. T. O'Leary, 'Indoctrination and the indoctrinated state of mind', p.80.

59. I do not wish to suggest that value judgements are made only in the fields of aesthetics, morals, politics and religion. Rather, my list is meant to serve as an illustration of the sorts of belief which are to be included in this category.

60. The question arises here as to whether a viable differentiation can be made between statements of fact and statements of value. Since a discussion of this problem lies outside the bounds of my paper, suffice it to say that I believe that the drawing of such a distinction is possible, and indeed warranted, in primary and secondary education. See for example, G. J. Warnock, *Contemporary Moral Philosophy*, Macmillan, London, 1967, pp.63-64.

61. D. Wright, *The Psychology of Moral Behaviour*, Penguin, Harmondsworth, 1971, p.158.

62. A. O'Hear, *Education, Society and Human Nature*, RKP, London, 1981, pp.123-124.

63. W. Hare, 'The open-minded teacher', *Teaching Politics*, Vol.5, No.1, 1976, p.30. Hare has italicized 're-opening'.

64. Such is also the case concerning those beliefs with which the very young child is indoctrinated.

65. Also included in category 'B' are those beliefs which it is unjustifiable to indoctrinate since they are expressed by propositions which are false. Examples are: 'Oscar Wilde was born in 1859', 'New York is situated on the west coast of the United States of America', 'the sun revolves around the earth', etc.

66. W. R. Casement, 'Indoctrination and contemporary approaches to moral education', Ph.D. dissertation, Georgetown University, 1980.

67. *Ibid.*, p.165.

68. *Ibid.*, p.168.

69. *Ibid.*

CHILDREN'S RIGHTS AND THE
JUSTIFICATION OF VALUES EDUCATION

Mike Bottery

The connection between children's right and the justification of values education may not be too apparent at first glance. However, this article will attempt to make this connection in four main stages.

(a) A conception of the 'child' will be advanced which suggests that most present conceptions are not sufficiently catholic to capture the huge diversity of capabilities and behaviours, or are too conservative in their estimates of children's potentials.

(b) The kinds of rights to which children should increasingly have access will be described.

(c) An assessment will be made of those arguments which purport to show that children should *not* have these rights. Crucial to this assessment will be the expanded and optimistic description of the concept of 'childhood'.

(d) Finally, by looking in detail at what is believed to be the strongest of these arguments, the limited rationality argument, and seeing why, in many respects, it fails, a view of values education will be arrived at which suggests the early and increasingly democratic involvement of the child, a respect and valuing of the child's opinions, and an appreciation that teachers and children are in many respects embarked upon the same journey.

But how, it might be asked, can a two-year old vote, learn to drive, or make decisions crucial to their welfare? The answer is that they can't. Children's rights can be a ridiculous idea. And it is normally with this kind of ludicrous example that the notion of children's rights is summarily dismissed.

Two things, however, should be noted about the above. Firstly, the person inclined to dismiss the concept of children's rights, should ask the question 'What is a child?' This surely is a crucial question, for within the simple term 'child' the present definition of childhood actually covers a wide age range from early infancy to late adolescence, and encompasses within it an enormous range of abilities, needs and potentials. If the 'child' is seventeen rather than two, then the notion of voting, driving or taking other important decisions makes much more sense.

Secondly, implicit in the argument against children's rights is the acceptance that if children *are* capable of exercising such rights then they should be allowed to do so. There are, then, strong similarities between arguments against children and other groups like blacks or women having rights. If a group is to be prevented from enjoying the same rights as the dominant group, then the first thing to do is to impugn their capabilities. If they are black, say that their IQ is significantly lower than that of whites – that they need to be treated in much the same way as children. Or if the disadvantaged group is one of women, argue that they are constitutionally, biologically, or temperamentally, unsuited to taking on the reins of responsibility that men normally have done in the past. If they are children, convey in the description of 'child' the idea of an emotionally immature, inexperienced, gauche, cognitively undeveloped person. Assert their incapacity and carry the argument. It is, therefore, very important to scotch this idea of there being one kind of 'child'. The variation is enormous, and one which a simple 'incapacity' argument cannot fairly counter without looking at individual cases much more closely.

Even granting this, one has to be enormously careful in the certainty of assumptions about children's capabilities. These tend to be heavily ingrained, and yet there has been a steady stream of developmental psychological material over the last fifteen years or so which suggests that 'children' are much more capable of complex logical and moral thinking than had been believed by Piaget[2], who still exerts an enormous hold over current thought in this area, Johnson[3], for example, showed that children of as little as eighteen months of age understood distress in another, and tried to do something about it. Borke[4] demonstrated quite clearly that children of 3 and 4 years are quite capable of understanding another person's emotions and the kind of face they would have such feelings. Both Hughes and Donaldson[5] have also shown that children of much the same age can take the cognitive perspective of another and imagine how another person would see things from a different angle from themselves. And Jahoda[6] has produced research to show that young children of six to eight years are very aware of what alcholic drinks look and taste like, of what sort of behaviour people exhibit when they drink in quantity. They clearly understand the concept 'alcohol' – strongly suggesting that education in this area could start much earlier than normally assumed. Furthermore, Davies[7] produces evidence to suggest that it is not so much 'children' who are incapable, in some biologically predetermined sense, but rather that it is adults who impose their definitions and assumptions of 'childhood' upon children, who then conform to these adult expectations, and consequently undersell their abilities. In similar vein, Mueller[8] found that three, four, and five-year-olds were more verbally explicit when communicating with a person who could not see, compared to one who could; whilst Shatz and Gelman[9] found a difference in the way in which four-year-olds speak to two-year-olds, and to adults, that was appropriate to the differential characteristics of the listeners. It is rather worrying to read a philosopher like Hobson[10], when considering methods of teaching rather glibly stating

In the early years it will be mainly a matter of instructing, with little in the way of intellectual backing or full rational explanation of what is taught . . .

. . . the assumption being that children can't understand such matters; and yet there isn't a single mention of any recent findings in developmental psychology. This kind of armchair philosophy enshrines existing dogma, and makes it that much more difficult to force a reappraisal.

Furthermore, since the seminal work of Aries[11], there has been a steady stream of historical literature suggesting that 'childhood' as such is not so much a biological event as a social construction, that 'childhood' as we know it is really an invention of little more than three hundred years, caused, depending upon one's point of view, by the emergence of an education system[12], changes from an extended to a nuclear conception of family structure[13], the rise of capitalism[14], or the increasing maturity of parents[15]. This emergence of childhood, it has been claimed, can be seen in such things as children being given special clothes distinct from adults; their having their own toys and games for the first time; a growing tendency to express in art children as children and not as miniature adults[16]; and a more friendly association of child with parent, characterised by a decline in the infant death rate[17].

To be fair, the evidence for the thesis is not conclusive. Pollock[18] has taken considerable pains to point out the inaccuracies, exaggerations and poor source material of many commentaries, suggesting that the historical thesis is at best not as strong as its proponents would claim. But even allowing for this, such a theory, like the findings in developmental psychological theory, does make one sit up and re-think one's comfortable assumptions about what a 'child' is. The answer to the question – 'what is a child?' – must of necessity remain incomplete, but the areas of incompleteness do point to the idea that 'children' are considerably more capable than present adult society believes. Within certain limits (to be discussed later), it would seem than an optimistic, experimental approach to their capabilities is the most appropriate.

So the summary dismissal of children's rights – in the liberationist' sense[19] – must be an unjustified one, and their consideration must have important implications for parents, teachers, the running of schools, and for society in general. If the principle is accepted that children should be granted certain basic rights, and at ages earlier than normally allowed, then these rights must affect the rights and duties of parents and teachers, and will throw an interesting light on present multicultural debates in this country.

These rights will necessarily suggest proper attitudes to values education for children. For example, if children have certain rights with regard to their development as autonomous beings, then education conducted in a didactic or indoctrinatory manner would· breach these rights. Hand in hand with this would go the argument that even when children had not reached a level of maturity which allowed them to exercise these rights, space should be left for their development. As Rawls[20] has argued, even were there a process for brainwashing people so that the outcome was that they would subsequently welcome their 'conversion', this would still not be morally justifiable. In like manner, just because children on 'maturity' may embrace with enthusiasm the doctrines and dogmas of the faith in which they have been schooled early in life, this does not justify the approach.

Instead, an approach to values education would be suggested which is tolerant and responsive to differences of opinion, and therefore allows the children to develop their own opinions within the framework of the school or the home.

Finally, if such an attitude to values education could be established, it will be found to harmonise in interesting ways with an attitude to epistemology in general, one which is aware of its tentativeness and changeable nature, is tolerant of criticism, is open-minded, and aware of its fallibility.

Do children, then, have any rights? There seem to be four rights in particular which adults in our society enjoy, which are denied or severely limited when applied to children. These rights are:

(a) the right to decision about their own actions;
(b) the right to decisions of dress and appearance;
(c) the right to expression of opinions;
(d) the right to involvement in institutional decisions which directly affect them, such as those in the family or the school.

Ranged against these rights for children, there appear to be five different arguments, which might be thus characterised.

(1) The Power Argument – that adults are stronger than children, and until children acquire the physical strength and mental prowess to compete with adults, they must pay due deference. Little time will be spent on this argument, other than to say that whilst it undoubtedly is the case that some people do act in accordance with this argument, I can think of no *ethical* argument to support their doing so.

(2) The Biological Relationship Argument – which argues that as the child is the direct inheritor of an adult's genes, the child is therefore dutybound to obey such a person. Implicit in the more extreme forms of the argument is the notion that children, because they are the product of a sperm and an ovum, are the property of the parents who produced the sperm and the ovum. The inevitable conclusion for such an argument would be, then, that the parents are the property of the grandparents, who are the property of the great-grandparents, until, no doubt, Adam

33

and Eve would own everyone alive today!

What this argument does suggest, though, is that where two people claim rights and duties to a particular child, the closeness of the biological relationship will normally be the determining factor in who will be given the decision, for it is usually the parents who will go to extraordinary lengths in time, attention and devotion to their particular child. It is a simple observation that parents do do these things, and therefore it is best for the child if they are given priority of interference. This is the point, I think, which Bridges[21] should be making when, instead, he talks of a 'moral trade-off' between parent and child – as if the demands of the child give the parents right of interference. The interference, however, is not *justified* on this argument – it is merely explained. Justification has to come from elsewhere.

(3) The Upbringing Obligation Argument. This might well be described in one outburst – '. . . and I've done my best for you since you were born, and this is how you repay me!' It suggests that the feeding, clothing, and caring of the child in the past gives the parent the right to determine the behaviour of the child in the future. It can be rebutted, I think, by another outburst – 'Well, I didn't ask to be born, did I?'; and surely it is unfair to suggest that obligations are due by anybody to anyone else in a situation where the person supposedly under the obligation never freely entered into the contract in the first place. The duties and attentions paid by the parent suggest at best an attitude of gratitude on the part of the child, rather than any relinquishing of rights – and gratitude is not a quality which can be created by demand, but rather by the relationship created with the child. Indeed, it might be that the kind of parental outburst quoted above, if used frequently enough as a means of extracting compliance from the child, would only be used by that kind of parent who had failed precisely in the creation of such a relationship.

(4) The Non-Contributory Argument. This suggests that because children have no financial stake in the running of the school or home, they should be debarred from decisions in their running. However, it might well be argued that it is precisely because they are financially dependent, that they are most likely to be affected by decisions, and therefore must have a say. This is not to deny that adults should have a large say – after all, it *is* their money! But arguments that adults have a better knowledge of value for money, of the ridicule that children may be subjected to if they choose outlandish clothes, and of the appropriateness of the materials for the weather conditions prevailing in that country, are, strictly speaking, nothing to do with the non-contributory argument at all – they are claims relating to children's limited Rationality, and we shall come to this now.

(5) The Limited Rationality Argument. Simply stated, this argues that because of children's immature, unrefined reasoning processes, and their

limited experience, their rights should be drastically curtailed. Now a number of problems immediately present themselves with this argument. Firstly, as noted at the beginning of this article, the developmental evidence suggests that children are much more capable than is normally credited. At the very least, the limited rationality argument must be tailored to such evidence. Secondly, there are enormous difficulties in simply determining when a child or an adult *is* capable. Is, for example, Piaget's[22] description of an abstract stage of reasoning in the human being the watershed for differentiating between child and adult? If so, then twelve to fourteen years would seem to be the age at which the changeover is made – an age that most adults in our society would think far too young. (Note that this is using research which is now increasingly seen as too conservative in its estimate.)

Even if criteria for 'mature' thinking could be established, it might be argued that it is the child's experience that is lacking. Here we are in a Catch-22 situation. Children may not be granted the right to gain experience because their experience is lacking! It is something of a truism to say that things are only fully understood when practiced. If many 'children' seem incapable of exercising rights, it may well be that this is not due to some biological immaturity, but more a combination of lack of experience and practice in such skills, and, more importantly, lack of belief in their ability to do so, precisely because the society in which they have grown up has fed them with the idea that they *are* incapable. This is *not* to suggest that the world is peopled with little supermen and superwomen, but rather to suggest that unless people adopt high expectations of 'children's' capabilities, and give them the opportunity (and the belief) to try such skills out, how shall we ever know?

A further difficulty with this argument lies in the fact that an adult may well have the required reasoning processes, but has lived so sheltered a life that they do not possess the range of experience which a particular 'child' has. There must be many cases, then, where adults (in the chronological sense of the word) do not meet any proposed criteria of reasoning and experience, whilst some children do. Wringe[23] describes this problem as the distinction between 'normative' and 'institutional' definitions of maturity. He suggests rightly that the normative definition is logically prior to the institutional: that determining who should be classed as an adult must precede the legal definition of adulthood. The complaint is that there must be many more cases at present than most people would credit where the institutional violates the normative.

Let us apply the limited rationality argument into a specific situation, that of the right of children to involvement in the institutional decisions of schools. And it may be as well at this point to divide the notion of 'institutional decisions' into two categories:

(a) decisions to do with the organisation of the institution – with its efficient running and management;
(b) Decisions to do with the curricula taught – with its composition, value orientation, and selection.

Regarding the first category, it is surely a deficiency in the running of the school if those taught are not consulted about the manner of their treatment, and about suggestions for improvement. The reactions and suggestions of pupils constitute an invaluable source of assessment material. As Barry and Tye[24] remark:

> If there is one lesson more than another which teachers (including heads) need to learn, it is to talk less and listen more . . .

Furthermore, not to consult children would be a failure to educate them towards democratic involvement within the community as a whole. This is not to advocate the wholesale transfer of power to the child; but it does argue that as children develop and mature, their suggestions may well be as insightful and valid as those of many adults – particularly as they are on the receiving end of much that goes on in school. It further suggests that their representation on various committees not only gives expression to these views, but also gives invaluable experience in participation. Finally, it gives a clear signal to such individuals that they are valued as people in the process of developing mature attitudes and views.

What, however, is one to make of the secondary category – the proposed right to institutional decisions with regard to the curricula? Much foolishness has been written on this issue, and the point by Moore and Lawton[25] is well taken:

> . . . teachers are, to some extent, *authorities* on what they teach . . . they must be authorities relative to those they are trying to educate . . . Pupils are not authorities in this sphere, since if they were they would not be pupils. There is thus a conceptual connection between *educating* someone and being an *authority.*"

This must undoubtedly be the case. The teacher does not have to be all-knowing or infallible to be an authority for the child. Broadly speaking, what Moore and Lawton are bringing out is the distinction between the aims and objectives of an educational enterprise. The objectives, the lesson structures, the short-term teaching strategies, are, as we have argued, very much within the capacity of the average child to criticise. Who better to judge the quality of the food than those who are eating it?

The aims, on the other hand, are the long-term goals, the ultimate ideals pursued by the teacher. This is an immensely sophisticated enterprise, combining as it does reflection upon different philosophical ideals, the application of psychological findings, a grasp of the range of relevant content areas, the use of practicable and effective implementation strategies, and an ability to apply relevant and workable evaluation techniques. A gradual education towards such an understanding should not be more beyond the capabilities of a teacher than the teaching of any other subject. Having said this, the fact remains that much of curriculum matters must be beyond the range of just about any child of any ability whatsoever. In this, they cannot be an expert or authority, and as such cannot expect to be consulted.

Having said this, there will come, very early in the child's education, situations which put the teacher on the spot, where they can either acknowledge that there is more than one opinion upon the matter at hand, that they are not all-knowing authority, or they can duck the issue and leave the educational aim of developing the child into a rational, questing, autonomous individual to some future teacher. What, for example, does the teacher answer when the child asks:

– does God exist?
– does grandma go to heaven when she dies?
– is it wrong to eat meat?
– is it wrong to fight wars?
– do we go to hell if we are bad?

These are questions which can be and are asked by the youngest of school-children. Much more is at stake than deciding between giving a quick 'yes' or 'no', which disposes of the question, or spending time on a more detailed answer. More important is the teacher's art and the child's autonomy – can he or she deal with this question in a manner which does not leave the child feeling marooned and adrift in a sea of uncertainties, but rather deals with the question in a way which begins to open up for the child the huge areas of human knowledge – some would say all knowledge – where no answer can be final and definitive, which introduces to the child the infinite wonder and variety, the uncharted depths of the mystery of human enquiry and existence? In all curricular areas where the subject under discussion is capable of different interpretations – in literature, in history, the social sciences, and the sciences themselves[26] – this element of individual interpretation can and should be introduced at the start, and not as some top-dressing, once the 'facts' are known.

The point is that if one of the aims of an educational establishment is to develop the child's sense of autonomy, then this must be recognised in matters curricular, as well as matters organisational. This is not just an epistemological point, but is a moral point as well. It is a child's right to be made aware of the differences of opinion, to know that an 'authority's' judgement is not the only one, and the acknowledgement of this right must inform the teaching of all subjects. This is not to undermine the authority of teachers, if by this is meant their greater degree of expertise in matters curricular when compared with the pupils. Nor is this to under-mine the overarching authority of logic and rationality which must apply for both pupil and teacher. It is to undermine, however, the authority of those teachers who *would* claim to be infallible and all-knowing. Teachers of values education have often felt under pressure because, unlike the teaching of other curricular areas, theirs has seemed to be either a meal of set dogmas or a menu of relativism. Neither viewpoint is satisfactory. An acknowledgement of children's rights suggests that respect for their developing autonomy and rationality, coupled with an understanding of the tentativeness and changeability of all curricular knowledge, come to-gether in a mutually reinforcing way. As children develop in understand-ing, so they can come to see that teachers, like themselves, are only seek-ers after the truth as well. The teacher may be further along the journey, and can thus point to some of the paths the child may take, and some of the pitfalls to avoid. But the teacher, like the child, is still travelling. This necessitates that as the child progresses, the teacher increasingly acknow-ledges the child's developing grasp of the nature of learning. The paradox of teaching seems to be, as Downey and Kelly[27] suggest, that 'the teacher's authority must contain within it the seeds of its own destruc-tion.' Any other form of education, in any curriculum area, which does not have such an aim, cannot be moral, and cannot be justified.

In the final analysis, the child will become an adult, and must take over the responsibilities within society that his parents and teachers hold at the present time. The greatest gift they can give to the child is the ability to cope with future difficulties. This can be done by providing the child with a secure emotional foundation, based on love and care, and a secure ra-tional foundation, based on logic and autonomy. In a world characterised by accelerating change, this cannot mean loading children with dogmas before they are ready to assess them rationally. It must mean an open-mindedness on the adults' part which allows children access to a variety of experiences, which broadens their outlook, and which enables them to understand others coming from different societies, value-systems and perspectives. The justification of children's rights provides the only kind of justification of values teaching, and that is an approach towards autonomy, based on care and rationality.

REFERENCES

1. R. Franklyn (Ed.), *The Rights of Children,* Basil Blackwell, 1986, Introduction p.7
2. (a) J. Piaget and B. Inhelder, *The Child's Conception of Space,* RKP, 1956.
   (b) K. Piaget, *The Moral Judgement of the Child,* Penguin, 1977.

3. D. B. Johnson, 'Altruistic Behaviour and the Development of Self in Infants', in *Merrill-Palmer Quarterly*, vol.28, no.3, 1982.
4. H. Borke, 'Interpersonal Perception of Young Children – Egocentricism or Empathy?'; in *Developmental Psychology*, vol.15, no.2, 1971.
5. J. Donaldson, *Children's Minds*, Fontana, 1978.
6. G. Jahoda, *Children and Alcohol: A Developmental Study*, HMSO, 1972.
7. B. Davies, 'Children through their own eyes', in *Oxford Review of Education*, vol.10, no.3, 1984.
8. E. Mueller, 'The Maintenance of Verbal Exchanges Between Young Children', in *Child Development*, vol.43, 1972, pp.930-938.
9. M. Shatz and R. Gelman, 'The Development of Communication Skills: Modifications in the Speech of Young Children as a Function of Listener', in *Monographs of the Society for Research in Child Development*, vol.38, 1973.
10. P. Hobson, 'Some Reflections on Parents' Rights in the Upbringing of Their Children', in *Journal of Philosophy of Education, vol.18, no.1, 1984, p.70.*
11. *P. Aries. Centuries of Childhood*, Jonathan Cape, 1962.
12. *Ibid.,* pp.306-7:
    The institutional development and acceptance of formal education in schools with the consequent isolation of the child from adult society, was a prerequisite of the emergence of modern sociological and psychological concepts of childhood.
13. E. Shorter, *The Making of the Modern family*, Collins, 1976.
14. M. Hoyles, 'Childhood in Historical Perspective', in M. Hoyles (Ed.), *Changing Childhood*, Writers and Readers Publishing Cooperative, 1979.
15. L. Demause, 'The Evolution of Childhood', in L. Demause (Ed.), *The History of Childhood*, Souvenir, 1974.
16. P. Aries, *op. cit.*
17. L. Demause, *op. cit.*
18. L. A. Pollock, *Forgotten Children*, Cambridge University Press, 1983.
19. R. Franklin, *op. cit.*, p.17, makes the necessary distinction between 'protectionist' rights and 'liberationist' rights – the former preventing the abuse of children, the latter allowing them greater freedom of action. Whilst this paper concentrates on the liberationist rights, this is meant in no way to detract from the need for protectionist rights. A balance between the two must be established – based on an understanding of children's capabilities and the things which threaten them.
20. J. Rawls, *A Theory of Justice*, Harvard University Press, 1972, p.197.

21. D. Bridges, 'Non-paternalistic Arguments in support of Parents' Rights', in *Journal of Philosophy of Education*, vol.18, no.1, 1984, p.60.
22. J. Piaget and B. Inhelder, *op. cit.*
23. C. A. Wringe, *Children's Rights*, Routledge and Kegan Paul, 1981, p.123.
24. C. H. Barry and F. Tye, *Running a School*, Temple Smith, 1975, p.98.
.25. M. Moore and D. Lawton, 'Authority and Participation', in D. Lawton et al. (Eds.), *Theory and Pracice of Curriculum Studies*, Routledge and Kegan Paul, 1978, p.262.
26. For a very readable account of the controversies going on in the very heart of a supposedly non-controversial area, see A. F. Chalmers, *What is this thing called Science?* Second Edition, Open University Press, 1982.
27. M. Downey and A. V. Kelly, *Theory and Practice of Education*, Third Edition, Harper and Row, 1986, p.124.

PASTORAL CARE
IN SECONDARY EDUCATION
Paula Stott

This article is an attempt to make explicit some of the issues underlying different approaches to pastoral care within the secondary school system.

Historical Development

In order to attempt any analysis of present-day patterns of pastoral care in our schools, it is necessary to locate its development within some sort of historical perspective. The difficulty of this task can be ascertained when it is realized that official publications on education before 1970 contain no specific reference to pastoral care as such.[1]

However, it is generally accepted that today's pastoral care has its roots in some of the nineteenth-century educational traditions especially those of church schools which concerned themselves with the child's spiritual and moral welfare, going beyond purely academic parameters. Boarding school tradition has also had an effect. Here teachers have had to assume roles and responsibilities beyond those of the classroom and have acted *in loco parentis;* this has, of course, extended itself to teachers in day schools in general and to those exercising pastoral responsibilities in particular.

The fact that the initial teacher selection for the expansion of the education system required that 'goodness and steadiness were much to be preferred to cleverness'[2] in the candidates substantiates McGuinness' claim that the aim of education was to help supply a basically educated workforce that would not use those skills for mischief. He argues quite convincingly that present-day education including pastoral care systems is still influenced by this nineteenth-century legacy.[3]

Closer to the present day, it is fairly true to say that pastoral care has come about more by accident than design, it has evolved out of necessity rather than being planned and carefully thought out as an approach to the nation's educational problems. The introduction of comprehensivisation has been directly responsible for stimulating the growth in pastoral care provisions. It is possible to categorise the reasons for this growth into three different, though related, areas.
1. Organizational
2. Professional
3. Personal

1. Organizational

Schools became much bigger, in some cases purpose-built, in others different schools joined together thus giving rise to the 'split-site' phenomena. This growth in size produced the need to 'collect, record and disseminate a great deal of information with a large number of pupils'.[4] The arranging of pupils into convenient class-size form groups greatly facilitated the performance of this task. Best, Jarvis, and Ribbins claim that even today pastoral care periods 'are actually provided to facilitate petty administrative functions such as marking the registers, reading school notices and collecting the dinner money.'[5]

2. Professional

Prior to comprehensivisation teachers had taught either in grammar schools or secondary moderns, now they were to be teaching in the same school, sharing the same staff-room. The problems of promotion and professional development had to be faced. Who were to be given scale posts? How were they to be selected? Best and Ribbins suggest that setting up formal pastoral care systems with paid posts of responsibility solved some of these problems.[6] What tended to happen with constant regularity was that grammar-school teachers became heads of academic departments and the newly introduced pastoral care structures became the province of the non-graduate teachers from secondary-modern backgrounds, or as Marland cynically though succinctly puts it, 'He looks good on the pastoral side tends to be used as a politer way of suggesting he's not much good in any thinking or leadership role.'[7] This development of separate promotion for separate structures contributed greatly to the pastoral/academic split which exists in so many of our schools today. It also unfortunately reinforced the superiority of the academic over the caring aspect of education.

3. Personal heads

Referring to 1. above, it is obvious that many of the larger schools posed potential problems in their pupil population. Students could suffer from feelings of anonymity, of isolation and of not belonging within large impersonal institutions. It was important therefore to find a means to counter this. So 'overtones, perhaps more imaginary than real, of comfort, protection and caring for individuals taken from elementary schools and public schools became interwoven into the structure of early comprehensives.'[8] This was achieved by dividing the school population into pastoral units and encouraging a sense of belonging. Theoretically, this would take care of the pupils' feelings of insecurity and give them an operational base from which they could negotiate their secondary school career.

However, it must be remembered that it was not just children who were suffering from reorganization, loss of status, change of role and of having to come to grips with complex and bewildering organizational structures; this also applied to teachers. Teachers were having to cope with feelings of insecurity and inadequacy in the face of working within new institutional frameworks, teaching pupils from different types of socio-economic backgrounds and developing staff-room relationships with staff from different academic and training backgrounds. The emergence of pastoral care structures could also do something to cater for the needs of the staff, but this is not always acknowledged and the implications not fully explored. (Some of the implications of personal needs of the teacher will be pursued later on in the article.)

Definitions of Pastoral Care

Prior to this point, the term 'pastoral care' has been used but it has not been defined; it now seems appropriate to attempt this task. The word attempt is used in recognition of the fact that the whole concept of pastoral care is remarkably resistant to consistent definition and its meaning is difficult to define accurately, indeed that 'pastoral care continues to be an enigma.'[9] The difficulty of definition is compounded by the seeming concreticity of the term, i.e. it is all to easy to assume that everyone understands what is being suggested when the term is used.

But how clear is the meaning of the term Pastoral Care? What is pastoral care aiming to do? Who is the caring for? Who does the caring? How do they do it? Should provision for pastoral care actually be located within a school framework and written into the job definitions of many teachers? The answers to these questions are *not* always uniform as pastoral care may (and often does) mean many things to many people. It is therefore imperative in professional discussion, or in planning of school policy, that terms are clarified, and aims and objectives are made explicit, and that the evaluation phase of curriculum planning is implemented, something sorely lacking at present. 'In more than half the schools there were no explicit criteria for the judgements being made about the effectiveness of the institution and the education being offered, particularly in issues relating to pastoral care.'[10]

In pursuit of a definition for pastoral care, it may be useful to examine how it actually operates within our secondary-school system; this leads to the conclusion that there is not just one definition but several, not just one use but in practice a variety of uses. This diversity signals a need for alertness, clear thinking and clear talking if confusion is to be avoided.

Definitions of pastoral care fall into several major categories and several major functions. These can be focused on

1. Needs of the school as an institution,
2. Needs of teachers,
3. Needs of the child as pupil,
4. Needs of the 'whole' child.

Each of these categories involve different value systems, different aims and in practice should involve different methods.

43

1. Needs of the School as an Institution

It has been suggested earlier that the pressing organizational needs of new comprehensives helped initiate pastoral care structures. These needs still pertain today. Bell and Maher make the point that in many cases 'the form tutor is left with precious little time to carry out pastoral duties and perceives this role to be secondary to meeting the demands of administration assemblies and staff meetings'.[11] It is therefore primarily a method by which the school can communicate with pupils about what is seen to be important in the day-to-day or year-to-year functioning of the school. Pupils can be kept abreast of the rules and regulations governing their lives. The exchange of information is almost always one way, i.e. from school to pupil or from school to parent. Information is disseminated about decisions which have been taken and with which compliance is usually expected. Pupils or parents are rarely engaged in any meaningful dialogue with the school and in so doing schools have 'cut themselves off too much from the most constructive feedback available to them, the feedback from the nature, needs and aspirations of the adolescents themselves.'[12]

It is also delegates parents to at best a peripheral role, with the result that

the parental dimension of pastoral care has been somewhat neglected by schools other than to regret the adverse effects of insufficient or uncaring parents.[13]

2. Needs of Teachers

Earlier, it was shown how some of the professional and personal needs of teachers were met by the introduction of formalized pastoral care into schools. How pastoral care meets some of the other needs of teachers will now be examined.

For teachers it can be a frightening experience to be faced with children and young adults who do not share their inhibitions. These teachers are sometimes out of their depth emotionally and therefore another major source of stress in teaching – disruptive pupils – is insecurity which is increased by the unpredictability of the pupil's behaviour.[14]

Dunham here draws our attention to some of the factors which can make the 'extraordinarily lonely profession of teaching'[15] even more difficult. We are given some insight into the fact that teachers have needs feelings and emotions; that they are taking part in a social interaction known as teaching and they will not be left untouched by that process.

Pastoral care systems go some way towards taking this into account but rarely explicitly. In its early days (and indeed still today) it partly acquitted this function by having teachers in pastoral roles who were disciplina-

44

rians and whose task was to 'sort out' problem children. Of course, in many cases this was also alleviating the immediate problem of the teacher. In this context, therefore, it is probably true to say along with Milner that 'pastoral care is a consciously evolved device for managing a potentially explosive situation which enables the teacher to remain in control.'[16]

This sort of pastoral care approach may actually alleviate the immediate problems of the teacher concerned, but will certainly not have helped him/her face/his own inadequacies of poor teaching or of poor classroom control. It functions as a protective devise whereby the problem is located in the child and it takes attention away from deficiencies in teachers and in the school that may be causing the problem behaviour.

It seems likely that the pastoral structures actually prop up and conceal the ailing academic wall of the teacher and school.[17]

The cost of this protectionism is often borne by increased stress levels of people in key pastoral roles within the school; this is due in part to the ambiguity of expectations and different functions they are expected to perform.

On the one hand I have to deal firmly and forcefully with a 15 year old bully and yet appear as a sympathetic approachable caring person to his classmate in need of help or advice.[18]

Teachers also need (like most humans) to feel wanted and to succeed, to have small groups with whom they identify. Pastoral care structures which involve teachers being responsible for a tutor group or form class cater for this need. Very often a great sense of identification occurs between teacher and class, teachers can be heard avidly discussing the merits of 'my form' or defending 'my class' against attack. This sense of bonding is quite often reinforced by naming the tutor group after the teacher concerned. This type of relationship can undoubtedly give a lot of satisfaction to the teacher but is also very demanding and needs adequate preparatory training, backed up by in-service training and support; a situation that unfortunately does not exist at present.

Holders of pastoral posts and those aspiring to them have been on fewer courses of any sort than others seeking promotion in schools, and the evidence of lists from L.E.A.s, D.E.S. and University Departments of Education is that there are far fewer courses specific to pastoral care available.[19]

This has been a brief attempt to identify some teacher needs which may be served through pastoral care in schools. It is a matter of some urgency that this area is more openly acknowledged and subject to investigation. This would help to guard against the danger that the hidden agendas of teachers may be producing a system that has more to do with their needs than those of the children they claim to be helping.

3. Needs of the Child as Pupil

Here the focus of attention is on the child as a pupil within the learning environment. The main aim of this type of pastoral care approach is to facilitate the learning process and to equip the child better to succeed in the academic life of the school. Douglas Hamblin promotes this model of pastoral care[20] and undoubtedly it has a lot of attractions for the teacher. It is seen as a way of reinforcing the central educative purpose of the school and may actually improve examination results by placing emphasis on areas such as study skills, improving learning habits, etc. This approach may be criticised on the grounds that it is too narrow and that pastoral care needs to be much more broadly based.

4. Needs of the 'Whole' Child

An increasingly important area of operation for pastoral care is that of the 'child centred' approach. The aim here is to make the needs of the child as a person (as opposed to the child as learner) central to the process and then to find ways of meeting these needs.

Within this approach to pastoral care there are two different methods of working which are not mutually exclusive and may in fact operate best when running in tandem. The two different orientations are (i) remedial, (ii) developmental.

(i) Remedial

This approach usually focuses on personal problems/difficulties and aims to help the child overcome these. This may involve the teacher in attempting to compensate for social or family deprivation, in other words to help the child overcome emotional problems whose origins lie far beyond the school gate, e.g. problems resulting from unemployment, poor housing conditions, divorce, death of a family member, etc. The teacher may be involved working on her own in a supportive or counselling way or she may liaise with outside agencies to obtain the help necessary. The main aim is to help the child overcome her emotional problems and to live more effectively, which in successful cases undoubtedly happens. However, all too often this type of pastoral care can be seen as inferior emotional first aid, or as an attempt by teachers to provide an extension of the welfare services through bungled attempts at counselling or amateur psychiatry. The end result may leave the child and family labelled as difficult or deficient in some way and the teacher (who may have had the best of motives) ends up feeling incompetent, frustrated and beaten.

Is this type of pastoral care 'assuming responsibilities which are more properly those of the family'?[17] If the answer is 'yes', then what gives schools the right to operate in this area? However, if it is 'no', and these areas should not be the concern of teachers, how can the child best be helped?

If it is accepted that schools have the right and morally should be involved in this type of work with children, then questions of selection and of training of teachers are inevitably raised, as are questions regarding relationships with other of the helping professions.

(ii) *Developmental*

The other approach to child-centred pastoral care is much less problem focused and is concerned with fostering the individual growth and personal development of each child. This is a very radical approach and suggests not that pastoral care should exist as an adjunct and a prop to the existing aims of the school but rather that the aims of pastoral care should be central to education. This would involve the re-shaping of existing curriculum, content and methods: 'Every school should create a pastoral curriculum to establish the concepts, attitudes, facts and skills which are necessary to the individual.'[22]

On the surface, this may seem very desirable and straightforward. However, on closer examination, various problems present themselves. It is pertinent to ask what are the concepts, attitudes, facts and skills which are necessary to the individual? The answer to this question is usually couched in fine-sounding though unspecific language. For example, the aim of pastoral care is to

(1) assist the individual to enrish his/her personal life;
(2) assist the individual to develop his or her own lifestyle and respect of others.

Rather than assume we know what the writer means, further difficult questions must be asked *and* answered. What exactly is meant by enriching? How do we know when someone is enriched? Is the enrichment to be mental, emotional physical?

Will schools, and that means teachers, seriously strive to help individuals develop their own lifestyle? How can this be achieved? What if this lifestyle entails a rejection of school and its values?

The above aims are specific examples of a pastoral care approach which is striving to increase the autonomy and independence of each pupil and to help each child achieve maximum potential.

At best, these types of aims are naively optimistic or at worst grossly hypocritical and deceptive given the view that 'in the final analysis whatever their ideals, their aims in practice are about getting pupils to obey authority and conform to social norms.'[24]

This perspective echoes the finding of T. Harris' polemical work[25] which locates education in a political context and argues very strongly that schools do little more than provide a capitalist society with what it needs. 'Teachers in general educate in that they act as agents of socialisation but they fail to Educate in the sense of going beyond socialisation to bring out and develop the full capabilities of their charges'.[26]

Given our existing system of social relations and economic production, could our society really tolerate an autonomous, independent questioning body of people educated to their maximum potential? Could our schools?

Undoubtedly some of the aims and methods of this approach to pastoral care are subversive, revolutionary even, in that they run counter to the prevailing ethos of our society. 'In this sense our Active Tutorial work is a kind of time bomb'.[27] The implications of this need to be openly acknowledged and examined, not just for pastoral care but for education as a whole.

REFERENCES

1. R. Best, C. Jarvis and P. Ribbins, *Perspectives on Pastoral Care,* Heinemann Educational Books, 1980.
2. G. Grace, *Teachers Idealogy and Control,* London, Routledge & Kegan Paul, 1978.
3. J. B. McGuinness, *Planned Pastoral Care,* McGraw Hill Books, 1982.
4. National Association of Pastoral Care in Education, *Preparing for Pastoral Care,* Warwick University Department of Education, 1986.
5. R. Best, C. Jarvis and P. Ribbins, *op. cit.*
6. *Ibid.*
7. M. Marland, *Pastoral Care,* Heinemann Educational Books, 1974.
8. A. J. Clemett and J. S. Pearce, *The Evaluation of Pastoral Care,* Basil Blackwell, 1986.
9. *Ibid.*
10. Her Majesty's Inspectorate, *Quality in Schools Evaluation and Appraisal,* DES/HMI, H.M.S.O., 1985.
11. L. Bell and P. Maher, *Leading a Pastoral Team,* Basil Blackwell, 1986.
12. J. Hemming, *The Betrayal of Youth,* Marion Boyars, 1985.
13. P. Lang and M. Marland (Eds.) *New Directions in Pastoral Care,* Basil Blackwell, 1985.
14. J. Dunham, *Stress in Teaching,* London, Croom Helm, 1984.
15. *Ibid.*
16. J. Milner, 'Pastoral Care: myth and reality', in *British Journal of Guidance and Counselling,* vol.11, no,1, 1983.

17. J. B. McGuinness, *op. cit.*
18. J. Dunham, *op. cit.*
19. M. Marland, 'Preparing for promotion in pastoral care', in *Pastoral Care in Education,* Basil Blackwell, vol.1, no.1, 1983.
20. D. H. Hamblin, *Problems and Practice of Pastoral Care,* Basil Blackwell, 1981.
21. J. Milner, *loc. cit.*
22. P. Lang and M. Marland (Eds.), *op. cit.*
23. M. Marland, *Pastoral Care,* Heinemann Educational Books, 1974.
24. J. Quicke, 'Charting a course for personal and social education', in *Pastoral Care,* Basil Blackwell, 1985.
25. T. Harris, *Teachers and Classes,* Routledge & Kegan Paul, 1982.
26. *Ibid.*
27. J. S. Pearce, 'Attitude, modification and evaluation: the pastoral curriculum', in *Pastoral Care in Education,* Basil Blackwell, vol.2, no.1, 1984.

VALUES EDUCATION IN ACTION – A DESCRIPTION AND JUSTIFICATION OF HUMBERSIDE THEATRE IN EDUCATION

This article was written mainly by Bill Seaman, the administrator for the company until the end of 1986, but with the help and agreement of the other members of the team.

Introduction

This article concerns the work of Humberside Theatre in Education (HTIE), a company committed to the development of the child's awareness of the problematical nature of value issues. A number of elements are seen as vital in this process. Firstly, the use of aspects of reason are involved – a demand for logic and rationality, for an understanding of underlying causality, and a heightened awareness of different perspectives on the same issue. Secondly, there must be an involvement of the emotions through such things as humour, pathos, and the kindling of empathy towards others' feelings and needs.

But thirdly, it is seen as vital that a linkage is made between these first two, for reason without emotional involvement is dry and uninvolved; emotional involvement without rationality is blind and unbalanced. This linkage is made through Theatre, by involving, the child personally in the ongoing drama and by maintaining and furthering the interest to highlight and examine the problems of the story. The child will not only find out many things about other people through Drama: with help they will find out much about themselves. The truth, then, is its own justification.

Theatre in Education: A Definition

Work done by professional actor/teachers in schools. Its primary aim is to use theatre and drama for educational purposes. Typically, it is done with one class or a specified maximum number of pupils for at least half a day. In addition to a play, a TIE programme may include some degree of active participation by the pupils. Most TIE companies tour within their own geographical areas: in Infants schools to Colleges. This local dimension is invaluable. It allows for close collaboration with teachers, responding to their requests for material as well as offering work of the team's own choosing.[1]

Company Policy

Humberside TIE aims to promote learning through personal and shared experience, where through the medium of theatre, young people can further their awareness of themselves and the world in which we live. The company aims not to duplicate the work already undertaken in schools, but to maximise the potential for this unique resource for learning by working with teachers to raise often complex moral, social and political questions with their classes.

Company Structure

While, for clear artistic purposes, the company has engaged either visiting or resident directors, policy making and educational direction is the responsibility of the whole company operating as a cooperative. Such collective responsibility, felt by many TIE companies to be essential to the content of the work, ideally allows each company member to contribute to the creative process from their unique educational and artistic backgrounds. The commitment and skills required to cross and combine the disciplines of drama and teaching result in the hybrid called the actor/teacher.

The stable company, therefore, consists of director, four actor/teachers and an administrator. In addition, many TIE companies ensure the development of the TIE programme after the immediate work with the actor/teachers by appointing a school liaison officer. Humberside TIE is negotiating with the Local Education Authority for a seconded teacher to fill this role which at present is undertaken by the director and administrator, in close consultation with a body of teacher consultants formed for this purpose.

Theatre and Education

There can be little doubt that theatre is a powerful medium for clarifying and communicating ideas. Effective theatre is accessible to its audience both in its choice of content and form, and through encouraging more people to use theatre for themselves to develop and communicate their own ideas. Theatre and education have much in common as processes of discovery and communication – Michael Attenborough argued at the Warwick Conference on Theatre and Education in 1984 – just as education which is out of touch with its pupils is bad education, theatre which is out of touch with its audience is bad theatre. At the same conference, Tim Brighouse, Chief Education Officer for Oxfordshire, spoke of the changing role of education and the role of TIE in this process.

> The challenge for education is to find ways of unlocking the confidence and creative capabilities of all young people. For many pupils, education is a mundane business of learning information and skills which can seem increasingly irrelevant to the lives they actually lead. The common result is a progressive loss of interest and self-confidence in the pupils resulting from the neglect of their indi-

vidual talents and abilities . . .
The curriculum is not solely in the schools. The curriculum is in the streets, in the home, in the work place and in the imagination. It is the backcloth against which the student acquires information, develops skills and attitudes, and encounters ideas. Of these, the last two receive less assiduous attention than we would wish. It is here that theatre has so much to offer education.

The Max Factor
A performance programme for twelve/thirteen-year-olds devised by the Duke's Playhouse Theatre in Education Company, Lancaster.

From the company's first year, 1983, it was felt to be expedient to adapt existing, proven TIE programmes in order to maximise the company's contact time with the full range of schools and thereby establish shared objectives and working relationships with educationalists across the country.

'The Max Factor' told the story of Kevin, a twenty-one-year-old with cerebral palsy. In a series of flashbacks Kevin powerfully illustrated how his severe handicap completely governed the way people related to him. His frustrations at home, in school and in social situations were detailed in deeply moving and often hilarious scenes. It was a production which challenged our attitudes and prejudices towards handicapped people – of particular relevance to Humberside's schools in view of the Authority's implementation of the 1981 Education Act calling for the integration of more handicapped children into mainstream schools.
Preparation: The company appreciated the necessity to gain firsthand experience of the lives of handicapped people, and consequently we regularly visited the local PHAB club (Physically Handicapped and Able Bodied club), forging a close relationship with Ron Walker. Ron suffered oxygen starvation at birth, as does Kevin in the play, and is consequently cerebral palsied.

The actor/teacher, who was to play Kevin, regularly visited Ron to discuss his life and the nature of his handicap. Ron invaluably assisted in movement and speech work, enabling the company to authentically reproduce the appearance and speech patterns of a cerebral palsy sufferer.

Further advice and assistance was forthcoming from parents of handicapped children, special schools, Education Authority advisors, the Educational Psychologists, Hull Royal Infirmary, and organisations for the handicapped such as the Spastics Society and Hull Disability Rights Advisory Service.

The company also hired Spastics Society films and read widely on the nature of handicap, each company member eventually choosing an area of research for the Teachers' Resource Pack to be evolved in parallel with the production during rehearsals.

Preparatory meetings were arranged at which the teachers concerned could experience the performance, receive the now completed Teachers' Resource Pack and discuss the potential of the programme and its applications in their schools. At these meetings the challenging nature of the programme was discussed at some length with particular reference to the impression it might make on handicapped children and their enhanced status within the school.

(a) The schools' tour

The schools were asked specifically not to prepare the children for the company's visit in order to maximise the effect of Kevin's opening entry. The seating and the set were arranged to bring the audience of sixty maximum in close proximity to the actors, and as Kevin moved with difficulty across the performance area, immediately in front of the children, a wide variety of responses were evoked – from open but uneasy laughter and an uncomfortable shuffling, through to a stunned silence. Leading from this powerful opening, a genuine empathy developed in this intimate setting between Kevin and the audience, with the children later writing,

It helped me to understand how disabled people must
feel about us and about themselves . . .

and

It makes you realise what they have to go through.[3]

Alan Orme as Kevin in a scene from 'The Max Factor' at
Greatfield High School, Hull, November 1983.

(b) Evaluation and responses

As an essential element of any programme, the company organises follow-up meetings for North and South bank schools to discuss the production's strengths and weaknesses, how teachers developed the stimulus and possible areas of future activity.

At the 'Max Factor' follow-up meetings, the power of the production to communicate was repeatedly stressed, as one teacher commented,

> The problems of the disabled were revealed in a way
> which could never be so clearly expressed in the classroom.

(c) Conclusion

For many children, 'The Max Factor' was their first experience of live theatre – and the power and proximity of the performance evoked deep emotions and 'immediate, lively and far-reaching' responses, which one teacher suggested had

> . . . made a lifelong impact on each member of the audience. Educationally, without over-sentimentality, a greater awareness of the lives of the disabled and disadvantaged has been promoted, as one thirteen-year-old explained,

> Before I thought that people like Kevin were stupid,
> I thought it was their fault they were handicapped.

Tim Brighouse identified a need for relevance to such TIE experiences:

> There is an urgent need for schools to engage openly and critically in the education of values. Specifically, they must tackle the issues and problems of individual and of institutional prejudice. Theatre in Education groups have an important role in schools and for the young generally – to enable them to see the effects of prejudice, rather than to replace one prejudice for another.[4]

The Burston Story

This was a full-day participation programme for one class of eleven and twelve-year-olds, devised by Humberside TIE.

'The Burston Story' was based on the remarkable events leading to the Burston School Rebellion of 1914. The children and parents of this small Norfolk village joined together to protest over the dismissal of their teachers, Tom and Annie Higdon. The action culminated in the villagers opening their own 'Strike School' building in 1917 in which the children of the village were taught by the Higdons for the next twenty-five years.

The company was committed, as far as possible, to accurately represent the events of the time and to capture the authentic emotions and motivations of those involved. Consequently, the company travelled to Burston to interview the only remaining villager who was a pupil at the time of the dismissal of the Higdons and who took part in the subsequent school strike. Also, much valuable research was done on the primary texts stored in the County Reference Library, Norwich.

During this historical research, the company discovered the many conflicting and partisan accounts of the events of this time, reflecting the struggle for and against change in the prevailing structure.

The aim, therefore, of 'The Burston Story' was to examine structure and change through the differing interpretations of events.

Following the period of research and discussion, the full day participation programme was devised by the company through improvisation linked to regular workshops with eleven and twelve-year-olds.

The preparation for and development of the day's activities are important elements in the programme of work. During this devising period the company also researched and compiled the Teachers' Resource Pack. This contained preparatory worksheets and information, notes on the company's aspirations for the programme, detailed background historical information, follow-up worksheets and suggestions for related activities, either for direct use with the class or for adaptation by the teacher.

The form of the programme owes a debt to our analysis of the methodology of Augusto Boal's Forum Theatre as adapted by Greenwich Young People's Theatre's version of these events in their programme 'School on the Green'.

Dave Broster and Pupils of Withernsea High School in a Scene from 'The Burston Story', April '86.

55

The theatre in the programme effectively raised complex moral, social and political questions which were then immediately synthesised and discussed in small groups. The form and content enabled the children to directly question the characters about their motives and to live through the dilemmas and conflicts of the children, parents and villagers of Burston, 1914. The children were each in a position to make decisions about their lives and, importantly, they were then to experience the consequences of the decisions they had taken.

It may be of interest to note what the D.E.S. document, *The Curriculum 5 to 16,* states on a similar point:

> No School can, or should seek to, conceal from its pupils the fact that there are moral questions on which people of equal integrity and thoughtfulness may reach quite different conclusions. But moral diversity does not make moral education impossible, still less unnecessary. It is right that the curriculum should help pupils to recognise and explore differences of view both about what people recognise as moral obligations and about what ultimately leads them to do so. Exploration of this kind contributes to the formation of pupils' own moral convictions.[5]

As one teacher observed in a letter to the company,

> The Burston Story presented two sides of an issue on which pupils were invited to debate. Too frequently, children are drawn emotionally to one side of an issue without being able to see the merit of counter argument.[6]

Two events in Burston in 1914 were primarily chosen as the vehicle for experiential learning. Nevertheless, we were at great pains to establish the historical accuracy of the programme in order for the children to learn of the complex and conflicting pressures for and against change in society. *The Curriculum from 5 to 16* states:

> In learning about people and how they live, pupils should be helped to appreciate that the present world grew out of the past. The themes which are studied should allow them to look for similarities and differences; to try and explain how and why change did or did not occur . . .[7]

The choice of this period is also important as 'The Burston Story' essentially was concerned with the lives of common people and their struggle for a voice. For, as the same D.E.S. document states,

> Choosing the content is a crucial matter since the act of selection and rejection can appear to confirm or deny the importance or significance of given groups of people, or or particular social, political and economic arrangements.[8]

56

Though 'The Burston Story' was not primarily created as a piece of historical drama, the programme nevertheless had an important contribution to make to the history curriculum. As Dr Stephen Baskerville from the University of Hull observed,

> I think this kind of production affords an ideal introduction to the whole range of historical problems and ideas: concepts which, with the age group for whom it has been designed, could hardly be addressed more effectively in any other medium or format.[9]

I hope that this summary of 'The Burston Story' illustrates that it was no 'day off', but was a rigorous, demanding and exciting day of learning through personal and shared experience, for all involved.

In Conclusion

'The Max Factor' brought many young people face to face with the world of a cerebral palsy sufferer. The programme graphically showed them the effects of prejudice but did so in a non-threatening way. It hopefully caused the audience to empathise with Kevin and to reflect on their own resistance to the lives of the handicapped.

'The Burston Story' was an experience for eleven and twelve-year-olds of the lives of adults and children from another region of the country, over seventy years ago. No overt parallels were drawn with today and no mention was made of current events. Nevertheless, the resonances of the programme will hopefully linger for many years to come, with the children making the connections between their own lives and those of the people of Burston. The evidence from Lynne Suffolk in her article, 'Theatre Memory and Learning – The Long Term Impact of Theatre in Education',[10] is that these hopes are very likely to be realised. Her study of the past programmes of Greenwich Young People's Theatre revealed,

> The evidence from the pupils in this case-study would indicate that the long-term impact of a TIE programme is considerable . . . in the main, pupils talked animatedly and in some detail about a programme they had experienced between one and four and a half years ago. In some cases recall of this 'one off' was more vivid after some four years than after a shorter time had elapsed.[11]

I hope that this article has served as an introduction to TIE and its exponents in Humberside. If knowledge of oneself and others – in thoughts and feelings – is a 'good' thing, then HTIE can be seen as furthering this development. It thereby aids the cause of examining problems with understanding and communication, rather than with ignorance and prejudice. This seems to be a more than sufficient justification for its work.

NOTES AND REFERENCES

1. **See K. Robinson (Ed.)**, *Theatre and Education – A Summary and Evaluation of a National Conference held at the University of Warwick, 20-22 July 1984*, Arts Council of Great Britain, 1985, p.5.
2. Speaking at the National Conference on 20 July 1984.
3. Personal correspondence with HTIE.
4. Speaking at the National Conference on 20 July 1984.
5. *The Curriculum from 5 to 16*, Department of Education and Science, HMSO, 1985, p.27.
6. Personal correspondence with HTIE.
7. Department of Education and Science, 1985, *op. cit.*, p.19.
8. *Ibid.*, p.19.
9. Private assessment written for HTIE.
10. L. Suffolk, 'Theatre, Memory, and Learning – the Long Term Impact of Theatre in Education', in *New Voices in Young People's Theatre*, No.15, 1986, pp.5-9.
11. *Ibid.*, p.5.

CONCERNING PEANUT BUTTER, RELIGION, MORALITY AND THE NATURAL LAW

Derek Webster

. . . and in my dream I saw Theology and Philosophy in the Areopagus. They were robed in the colourful dignity of female professors. With them was a rather pale undergraduate.

'You see,' Theology was saying, 'religions offer rich avenues for moralists. Religious people see their God as a moral Being. This affects the ways in which they relate to people. Some of them will feel committed to particular patterns of discipleship and may wish to tithe, give alms or engage in works of mercy.'

'A friend of mine', said Philosophy thoughtfully, 'was impressed by these patterns for living among believers. He used to argue, though, that Christian religious convictions were, at hearts, simply intentions to act in special ways.[1] He felt that the person who declared that God was love was really stating his determination to live life in a loving manner. The scriptures he took to be stories which embodied and backed up ways of living.'

The undergraduate, feeling that this might be useful for her final examinations, took out her note-bok and jotted down a couple of questions.

Do religious statements announce allegiance to moral principles?
Can they be assimilated to moral assertions?

Then she smiled to herself as she recalled a sixth-form debate on Matthew Arnold's view that religion was 'morality tinged with emotion'.

After a pause, Theology said, 'I think your friend is wrong. His view makes a mockery of "the faith of the Saints and the Fathers".[2] When a believer says that God is love she isn't just affirming a way of living. She is committing herself to facts found in the New Testament. These facts comprise the essence of her faith and also serve to explain Christian morality. It matters that these facts are true. To view them as helpful because they offer stories of moral inspiration ignores the question of their truth.[3] It puts the New Testament in the same category as *Pilgrim's Progress* or a Patience Strong calendar. You might remind your friend that St. Paul faced this question when he wrote in a letter to the Corinthians that "if Christ has not been raised your faith is futile".'[4]

Philosophy did not wish to argue her friend's case. She said, half to herself, 'Anyway, if he thinks that religious language is only meaningful when expressing moral intent, I wonder how adequate his understanding of meaning is.'

The student, who had just caught this, quickly scribbled down another question.

Is the empiricist's principle of meaning flawed?[5]

'As you might expect,' said Theology to the student, 'I would want to say that it matters that God is a moral Being when people decide how they should live. But I wouldn't want to resist an argument for the independence of morality and religion by agreeing that the first subsumes the second. This seems to be what Philosophy's friend is inviting us to do.'

After a much longer pause, Philosophy said, 'I wonder, is a believer's behaviour good because God commands it or does God command it because it is good?'[6] The undergraduate looked up at her quizzically. Philosophy explained. 'Well, if behaviour is good because God commands it, then morality is quite arbitrary, is dependent on divine whim. So when God commands the sacrifice of a boy, perhaps like Isaac, this becomes right and good.[7] On the other hand, when behaviour is commanded because it is good, morality becomes antecedent to and independent of God, yet binding for him. Morality thus brings God under judgement: this believers hold is blasphemous.'

'Hmm,' mused Theology, 'I am not going to sit on either horn. The dilemma supposes that the good and God are related only through dependence. In the relationship one is always derived and the other always sovereign. This is a presupposition I don't have to make. I don't think that moral qualities are "unanalysable atomic units" to be put either here or there, to be either wholly independent of or wholly constituted by God.[8] What the religious person understands by God is a Being whose ultimacy implies absolute goodness as an intrinsic attribute. God then necessarily acts with absolute goodness: his will and the good are identical. It has been well said that

God, by the necessity of his immutable nature, wills only what is good; so in obeying him one is aiming at the good for its own sake.'[9]

Theology waited for a few moments. As neither Philosophy nor the student seemed inclined to comment, she went on. 'Many believers think that God's laws can be perceived through their thinking.'

At this the undergraduate grinned. Much to her surprise she had remembered a fragment from the previous year's reading. She quickly scribbled:

Hobbes: God declareth his laws by the dictates of natural reason.

Theology went on, 'Rational thought offers a means to determine right from wrong. This natural knowledge is used to reflect on and analyse religious claims, scriptural injunctions and divine revelation. But such human judgment does not render God susceptible to some external and

60

prior moral thraldom. Human rationality with its knowledge of good and evil is itself part of God's creation and a reflection of his will.'[10]

Again there was a long pause. Then Philosophy said, 'Let me take up another point. Clearly you wish to make a link between what you say God is and how you feel believers should act. But that looks to me as if you are committing the naturalistic fallacy.' The student's brow furrowed slightly so Philosophy said to her. 'When a believer says that God is a forgiving Father he is making a purely descriptive statement about God. When he goes on to claim that therefore he must behave in a forgiving way, he is making a moral judgement. However, it is illegitimate to move from a view about what is the case to what ought to be the case. So it may be that donkeys are starving in Somalia. No moral implication about how I should act follows from this any more than it does from other descriptive statements, like donkeys in Somalia have long ears.'

Theology said slowly, 'I think that some descriptions of situations can imply moral obligations. If a woman ran up to me in the street screaming, "My baby is choking to death," that may well be a perfect description of what was happening. It carries with it the thought that I have a duty to help if I can. More importantly, however, is the point that it does not work to regard statements like God is a forgiving Father as if they were the same as Mr Brown, my next door neighbour, is a forgiving father. Statements about God are not exactly the same as statements about one person among other persons. They concern that transcendent to whom a person's existence bears only a distant, though still real, analogy. So, be-, cause of what is meant by God, the naturalistic fallacy does not apply. Certain things that can be said about him communicate both what is the case and what ought to be the case.'

'So you imagine that lets you off the hook, do you?' queried Philosophy. 'God always seems to be the exception standing beyond the rules of logic. You pay a high price for this in that the links between state-. ments about God and the language of ordinary human living become very tenuous.'

'It is a difficult problem,' agreed Theology. 'Why don't we join forces and conduct some advanced classes for the postgraduates on the structure and logic of religious language?' The undergraduate looked crestfallen.

Philosophy did not pick up the suggestion. She was overworked already on too many committees, trying to solve the financial problems besetting the university, without taking on extra classes – even on God-talk.

'Look,' she said rather briskly, beginning to pick up her papers and put them in her brief-case, 'shouldn't you accept where all of this is leading? You say that the analogy between the life for us and God's life, between our behaviour and thinking and his behaviour and thinking is very distant. So you are in no better position than the rest of us with what you can know and say about God. Your talk about him never turns out to be clear,

61

literal or straightforward. It doesn't submit itself to the usual tests of verification or falsify . . .'

'Oh dear, not all that again,' said Theology, interrupting in mock weariness.

'Admit it,' pressed Philosophy, 'you should really embrace agnosticism. Indeed quite a few scholars I know would ask you to concede more. They find no sound arguments for the existence of God. They view the problem of evil as insuperable if God is all-loving and all-powerful. They hold that increasing knowledge makes the God hypothesis superfluous.'[11]

Theology pondered awhile and then admitted rather ruefully, 'It's true that human goodness and divine goodness are far apart. If you and I had the tongues and the wisdom of angels we would be a little better at grappling with these difficulties. Certainly as humans we shall never reach very far to God. And if that was all there was to it I would be more agnostic than I am. However, he may stoop to us, talk with us and deal with us if he so chooses. He may even become man. In the Athanasian Creed . . .'

Philosophy cut in, saying, 'My dear, this is sheer dogma and will have to wait for another time.' With that she swept away towards the Senior Common Room in the far corner of the Areopagus, from whence there came the tinkling of china tea-cups.

'I think that I have upset her again,' said Theology to the student as she sat closer to her. Leaning back on one of the stone columns, she took a Tupperware lunch box from a very bulky brief-case.

'What is your name?' she asked.

'Damaris,' came the shy and rather surprised reply.

'Well, Damaris, do put your note-book away. Let's just talk like human being. Have a peanut butter sandwich.'

They munched for a few minutes, then the student said, 'I was surprised at something you mentioned a bit earlier. You said that rational thinking gave us the means of telling right from wrong. You claimed that religious prescriptions, scripture and revelation were subject to it. I would have thought that you would have relied on authorities like the Bible, the church, the Pope or revelation instead.'

'I think that it does surprise quite a few,' Theology said. 'People do still sometimes imagine God to be a rather crusty, uptight and elderly colonel issuing his moral instructions in the Ten Commandments. Yet many Christians prefer to take as a starting point for moral thinking the fact that we are all human. They argue that the demands of morality arise from a person's nature, from the very structure of a person's being. It seems to be a view which St. Paul takes in a letter which he wrote to Rome. He argued that

> When Gentiles who have not the Law do by nature what the Law requires, they are a law to themselves, even though they do not have the Law. They show that what the Law requires is written on their hearts . . .[12]

Some have thought that this is what Jesus of Nazareth meant too when he asked the crowd, "Why don't you judge for yourselves what is right?"[13]

The student looked puzzled. She thought to herself that is she had her note-book out she would have written:

Man's obligation derives from man's being.

Then she said, 'There really is a lot that I can't understand about this. How can we know what our nature is; and then what does that nature consist of? How does it imply a morality; and what would that morality be?'

Theology looked at her rather seriously. 'If you are interested in questions like this, why not come to my philosophy of religion seminars each Monday afternoon this term? The questions are too complex to answer quickly. But it might help if I sketched the views I'd be developing in those seminars.

'So to take your first question, I think that we can know about our town natures through a transcendental deduction. Knowledge gained in the world through our senses and experiences is "a posteriori" knowledge. It is what concerns us in spatio-temporal living when we learn how to do a baby's nappy or make Irish stew. Yet on reflection this knowledge presupposes, as the very condition of its possibility, an ultimate grounding.'

She reached into her brief-case and pulled out a book. 'I am reviewing Father Otto Muck's book, *The Transcendental Method.*[14] You might care to borrow it from the library. It argues very convincingly that a metaphysical understanding of being is implied by experiential knowledge. It is by this route that we may find that we come to some understanding of our natures.'

'I think that Philosophy would see this as a very tricky move,' commented the student rather uncertainly.

Ignoring this, Theology went on, 'Another of your questions was about human nature itself.'

'Yes,' said Damaris. 'Are you saying that it is always the same? If so, how do you explain that people change? The sheer variety of cultural forms, both now and in the past, shows how different we are.'

'Indeed,' nodded Theology, 'but independent of historical contexts and underlying the richness of all cultures is the metaphysical nature of human beings. It is what necessarily belongs to them at all times.[15] When we move from the activities of people in their living and reflect on what is necessary for the possibility of such activities, something of this nature becomes evident. We discover in human conduct the universal principles of obligation which are part of our natures. Such principles are sometimes called the natural law. When you ask what sort of a morality is implied by our nature, you are really asking a question about the content of natural law.'

'Hmm,' said Damaris. She was exasperated that so much was unexplained. Then she said, "It sounds to me as if God is a transcendental engineer who has planned man's moral course beforehand and then embedded this plan into each person's nature.[16] What is this plan?'

There was a short silence, then Theology said, 'If I had the time to develop my ideas I hope that I could persuade you that such a view is a distortion. It implies a static determinism with which I would not agree and a precision about natural law which is just not evident. Further, it isn't necessary to introduce the word God. Our starting point is man, not God. This offers a wide common ground. So the natural law foundation of morality, although it does in my opinion lie behind Christian morality, "may be the same as the foundations of the moralities associated with other faiths or with non-religious beliefs".[17] But to answer your question. The word plan is misleading. The content of the natural law stems both from that rationality which man discovers within himself as a fundamental "given" and from a transcendental "oughtness" which draws him to realise the fulness of his humanity in living. From these primary insights develop, not a tight code of eternally valid and clearly enumerated laws against which all other codes and moralities may be judged once and for all, but guidelines or, perhaps better, a direction.

'I have suggested that behind the changes in cultures through history the structure of the human nature remains the same. Really, this is only half of the truth for the structure of human nature is open and dynamic. It strives for fulfilment and so is capable of change at its most fundamental level. As it unfolds in the movement towards its unknowable future we have to revise our insights. Now the natural law, this direction for conduct, will never be pinned down finally because the nature of man cannot be finally grasped. We stand within time, so present knowledge of natural law is inevitably historical. Obviously, then, this knowledge can change as contexts for living, as man himself and as our insights change.'

'But I still don't know what the content of the natural law is,' insisted Damaris.

Theology smiled. 'There are good arguments for suggesting that the structures of human nature from which the natural law derives are very general ones. Ultimately they promote the preservation and fulfilment of life.

'Firstly, they involve people moving outwards towards others to establish positive and life-affirming relationships. So the egoist who seeks to subdue everything and everyone to his own purpose diminishes his humanity.

'Secondly, they imply a "having' which is sufficient for the realisation of potential and yet which is also responsible and correlated with duties to those who have less.

'Thirdly, they prompt a sensible regard for the body as the medium through which sustaining relationships are possible. Over-indulgence on the one hand and too rigid an asceticism on the other represent the denial of a proper humanity.

'Fourthly, they affirm the social nature of man for it is within community that his being is truly enhanced.

'Fifthly, they call man to resolve his spirituality. The question of God is part of the grammar of his being and is always with him in one form or another.

'Finally, they enable men to identify what is evil and destructive of their humanity.

'These, then, are the "basic characteristics written into the context of human life which mean that we cannot make of it whatever we choose".[18] They constitute "the parameters of human freedom".[19] Catholic moral theology is insistent that, if human responsibility is to have meaning, moral truth must be available prior to revelation.'

Theology stopped for a moment, then said quietly, 'Many Christians would argue that there is a continuity between the natural law and the revelation that is given within their faith. Father Newman puts it well when he points out that moral vision is enlarged and confirmed by the teaching of Jesus of Nazareth.[20]

> There is, perhaps, no greater satisfaction to the Christian than that which arises from his perceiving that the revealed system is rooted deep in the natural course of things, of which it is merely the result and completion.

'As for the natural law, then, its content is never finally established – for this would place it within history and render it susceptible to social conditioning. It stands simply as "the criterion that is ontologically prior to every positive law".'[27]

There she stopped. Damaris thought for a long while. Then she said, 'I have problems with so much of that that I will come to your seminars. And I still think that tucked away in all of what you have said God lurks, ready perhaps to be produced – like the rabbit from the magician's hat – in case you need an authority.'

Theology laughed. 'Look, if we are to talk authority and authorities, I'll have to have a drink. Peanut butter sandwiches always make me thirsty. Do you think that the tourists will have gone by now?'

As they moved slowly off, the statue of Denys the Areopagite came to life. He flung on a tunic and took them both to the now empty cafeteria. Theology could be heard saying, 'There are, of course, certain circumstances when it is quite legitimate to appeal to authorities. If you read Hughes' book on just this, perhaps as a Lenten exercise, you might find that . . .'[22]

NOTES

1. R. B. Braithwaite, *An Empiricist's View of the Nature of Religious Belief,* Cambridge University Press, 1955.
2. A. N. Flew, *God and Philosophy,* Hutchinson, 1966, p.23.
3. E. L. Mascall, *Words and Images,* Longmans, 1957, pp.49-62.
4. 1 Corinthians 15: 17 (New International Version).
5. D. A. Pailin, *Groundwork of Philosophy of Religion,* Epworth, 1986, p.200.
6. Plato, *Euthyphro,* 8b-10a.
7. Genesis 22: 1-19; also S. Kierkegaard, *Fear and Trembling,* Oxford University Press, 1939.
8. J. L. Mackie, *Ethics,* Penguin, 1977, p.230.
9. K. Ward, *Rational Theology and the Creativity of God,* Blackwell, 1982, p.177.
10. A. O'Hear, *Experience, Explanation and Faith,* Routledge & Kegan Paul, 1984, p.72.
11. K. Nielsen, *Contemporary Critiques,* Macmillan, 1971.
12. Romans 2: 14-15 (Revised Standard Version).
13. Luke 12: 57 (New International Version).
14. O. Muck, *The Transcendental Method,* Herder & Herder, 1968; J. Donceel (ed.), *A Marechal Reader,* Herder & Herder, 1970.
15. K. Rahner (ed.), *A Concise Sacramentum Mundi,* Burns & Oates, 1975, p.1020.
16. R. A. McCormick, *Notes on Moral Theology 1965–1980,* University Press of America, 1981, p.132.
17. J. Macquarrie, *Three Issues in Ethics,* SCM Press, 1970, p.90.
18. M. Wiles, *Faith and the Mystery of God,* SCM Press, 1982, p.109.
19. J. Macquarrie, *In Search of Humanity,* SCM Press, 1982, ;.135; I am especially indebted to Chapter 11.
20. J. H. Newman, *University Sermons,* SPCK, 1970, No.2, p.31.
21. J. Macquarrie, *In Search of Humanity,* SCM Press, 1982, p.137.
22. G. J. Hughes, *Authority in Morals,* Heythrop Monograph, 1978; also K. Ward, *The Turn of the Tide,* BBC Publications, 1986, Chapter 4.

Note: I wish to express thanks to the shade of Austin Farrar for the idea behind this little piece. His disciples will know that I have filched it from his 'A Theologian's Point of View', *The Socratic,* 1952, No.5. I only wish that I better served his wisdom and impish humour. (I would also like to thank Mrs M. Tickner for her valuable assistance in the preparation of this article.)

D.W.

NOTES ON CONTRIBUTORS

Mike Cross is Director of the Moral Education Centre at St. Martin's College, Lancaster, and Editor of the Moral Education Journal 'Values'. Before St. Martin's College, he taught in Secondary Schools in Derbyshire, and has for a number of years been involved in Inservice Training for Teachers.

Patrick Costello is a Lecturer in Educational Studies at the University of Hull. His principal research interests are the Philosophy of Education, the primary and middle years of schooling, Moral Education, and the teaching of philosophy to children.

Mike Bottery is a Lecturer in Educational Studies at the University of Hull. He has taught in primary schools in England and Australia, and his interests include the Philosophy and Psychology of Moral Development, and teaching strategies in Moral Education in the primary school.

Paula Stott is a Lecturer in Educational Studies at the University of Hull. She has had a varied teaching career in both secondary and further education. She has also worked as a counsellor and a tutor with the National Marriage Guidance Council. One of her special interests is in Personal and Social Education in Schools with particular regard to the function this fulfils for both teachers and pupils.

Humberside Theatre in Education is a full-time professional theatre company established in 1983. The company receives funding from Humberside Education Authority and Lincolnshire and Humberside Arts, enabling it to offer a free educational theatre service to the region's schools. Presently, the company consists of a Director, Administrator, and four actor teachers.

Derek Webster is a Lecturer in Educational Studies at the University of Hull. His particular interests at the present time are concerned with religious education, creativity, and the imagination.

BOOK REVIEWS

Staff Development in the Secondary School: Management Perspectives
Edited by Chris Day & Roger Moore. Pp 312
Beckenham: Croom Helm Ltd, 1986. pbk £9.95.

This collection of articles is both timely and ambitious. It is timely in its concern with staff development and appraisal given central government's declared interest in the appraisal of teachers and also in view of the new funding arrangements for INSET. It is ambitious in its stated objectives of both improving management practice by helping the trainers to focus their courses appropriately and in aiming to encourage those involved in school management to approach their work more purposefully.

The opening articles by Elizabeth Ballinger and Joan Dean set the management of staff development into the context of the needs of secondary schools to develop skills of human resource management and of LEA enabling policies whereby appraisal might be linked with individual development in the context of LEA management policy. These two chapters, taken together, provide a unifying thread for the remainder and introduce associated skills of time-management, inter-personal relationships and target-setting which are taken up in varying degrees and from different perspectives in the remaining articles. Sub-themes are the importance of participative management, in schools, of staff development and appraisal, and, perhaps most important, of the provision of the required supporting INSET; the importance of starting with an assessment of the needs of the individual teacher and the individual institution in designing in-service provision; and the need for training in evaluating those needs for all concerned. Robert Moon's concluding vision of the future usefully avoids the common confrontation between 'top-down' and 'bottom-up' models of what must, in the end, be a collaborative venture between the schools, LEAs, higher education, industry and commerce by proposing a model in which negotiation of needs and provision is the key element.

At the practical, enabling level of the roles of Heads, Deputies and Heads of Department in their own schools' approach to staff development and appraisal perhaps the most important concern developed in the book is that of time-management as a pre-condition of their ability to assume a management role in relation to others. Of particular interest also to those involved in organising management courses for senior staff in secondary schools, and to the present reviewer, currently involved in organising one such course with a substantial in-put from 'outside' education, is the book's assessment of the relevance to school management of insights available from industry, commerce and elsewhere. Cogent arguments are presented for the essential transferability of approaches and techniques developed there to the management of a school as a complex organisation. Industry's potential contribution to the more effective management of schools, and particularly to staff development and appraisal, has yet to be fully appreciated.

On reading this book one cannot fail to be impressed by the fund of commonsense and good-will among the several partners to effective in-service work represented here, which is essential to the success of staff appraisal as an integral aspect of a comprehensive and carefully designed staff development policy which meets the needs of the schools and LEAs. Appraisal, in that wider context, can be a golden opportunity to enhance the professionalism of the teaching profession. However, given the new funding arrangements for INSET, which provide at least the opportunity for LEAs to determine the direction and style of in-service support, only time will tell whether the envisaged partnership will come about. Only time again will tell whether the book's wider ambitions are achievable, however, its immediate value, from a trainer's perspective, lies in its dispassionate account of what has already been done and as a source of practical ideas.

B. V. Spence
Institute of Education
University of Hull

Preventing Classroom Disruption: Policy, Practice and Evaluation in Urban Schools.
By David Coulby and Tim Harper.   Pp.189
(Croom Helm, 1985) £7.95.

David Coulby and Tim Harper do not believe in mincing words. At the outset (p.3) they wish "to assert boldly that there is no such thing as a disruptive pupil." Before the practising teacher recoils in horror and asks them if they have ever been in a school, they go on to explain that the term 'disruptive' should be applied to specific behaviours and situations, rather than to pupils. By making this distinction they hope to prevent children from being seen as having something permanently wrong with them, as being mentally ill in some way, and thus of discouraging the view that the situation is one about which little can be done.

By focusing our attention on behaviour and situation, they claim, not only do we move away from perceiving disruption as unchangeable, we also objectify the problem – we can list and quantify specific behaviours which count as disruptive. Once we have agreed upon what counts as disruptive behaviour (and this, they concede, will vary from teacher to teacher), then through discussion and consultation, policies can be adopted aimed at reducing the levels of disruptive behaviours. Whether these policies are successful or not can be evaluated at the end of an agreed period, employing the assessment techniques used at the beginning of the referral, and comparing scores.

Such an approach can be rather offputting, but it becomes clear that the authors do not reduce individuals to lists of behaviours – there is a humanity running through the book which is, perhaps, surprising after the book's polemical first pages.

The authors suggest that there should exist within local authorities a special team of peripatetic teachers trained in dealing with such situations who are called in by the school not only as fresh minds and cool heads to assess the problem, but who can also suggest specific remedies and their implementation. They argue, and I think quite convincingly, that such a team of educational paramedics would be better utilised in a peripatetic capacity than as individuals located permanently within particular schools, though they are at pains to point out the problems which any relatively low-status young outsider has in gaining respect for his opinions. From the copious case material they present throughout the book, it is apparent that they have an approach which to some extent *depends* on being an outsider. Their open-mindedness, ability to apply their skills where most needed, and sheer intellectual energy to deal with difficult cases, may well be watered down by confinement to one campus.

Coulby and Harper are therefore suggesting a model of working which has five main components – referral, assessment, formulation, intervention, and evaluation – which examine the behaviour of disruption and attempt to change the frequency of that behaviour. They are at pains to point out that they are looking for solutions primarily within the school: in other words, that one removes the disruptive behaviour by changing the skills, organisation, or flexibility of the teacher and the school. Before their minds is an image of Procrustes' bed: we must change the shape of the bed rather than the shape of the child. The viewpoint is put most forcefully at the beginning of the book, and, I think, probably too forcefully. One isn't quite sure whether the authors are blaming teachers for inadequate teaching which thus produces disruptive behaviour, or whether they are saying that regardless of any cause, the one place that teachers can do something about behaviour is in the classroom, and so that is where teacher intervention must take place, or, indeed, whether the school must respond to new demands by changing its approach. At a time when teacher morale is as low as it has ever been, a book which begins by appearing to locate disruptive behaviour at the feet of inadequate teaching is hardly likely to get a considered reaction from practising teachers, and is likely to be utilised by some people for purposes very different from those intended by its authors.

It is unfortunate that the book could be interpreted in this manner, for it has many virtues. Not least of these is the positive manner in which it argues that those children exhibiting disruptive behaviour should be given the status of having special educational needs. Segregating them off into special units not only institutionalises the idea of such children as being different, and thereby intensifies perceptions about them, but it also runs counter to the philosophy of integration which permits the child a greater understanding and tolerance of his peers through working with them, but which also demands of the teacher more varied and flexible teaching skills.

Ultimately I think the book must be seen within this integrative perspective, and the book's prescriptions as being means to achieving these ends. To this extent, David Coulby and Tim Harper have produced a valuable and stimulating piece of work. Of course, such prescriptions need to be backed by hard cash and a teaching force which does not feel threatened, and it may well be the lack of both which results in the philosophy of integration not being fully realised.

Mike Bottery,
Department of Education,
University of Hull.

Educational Conflict And The Law
By David Milman. Pp. xxii + 145
(Croom Helm, 1986) £16.95.

This work, not counting content pages, consists of 171 pages of which only 113 consist of the actual text. In other words one third of the work is given over to Guides, Tables, Footnotes and Index: a by-product of the new technology for which all words are the same and tables and footnotes cannot readily be reduced. The size of the scholarly infra structure might lead to the view that the work is a basic text. The author, however, disclaims any such intention, as he does that it might be a handbook for teachers. His intention is to stimulate an interest in the relationship between Law and Education and to highlight (or chronicle) "current trends in the field of education law."

He sets out to achieve his objectives by a description of educational institutions and the sources of education law. Successive chapters then deal with state schools, the independent sector, parents and educational conflict, children, teaching personnel, legal issues in tertiary education and an evaluation.

The approach is not Olympian. A plan (to revitalise the nursery education programme) "suffered a setback with the savage education cuts in the late 1970s" (p.6). In discussing milk, meals and transport (as ancillary to the basic duty of an l.e.a.) he writes "unfortunately, it is because of this that they have become the targets of economies" (p.11), and on the decisions to publish HMI reports on schools he declares "This public relations move appears to have rebounded on the Conservative Government because many HMI reports have highlighted the damaging effect of education cuts . . ." (p.19). There are also some signs of the use of journalese not necessarily appropriate to a serious study of the use of legal process in education conflict, eg the reference to Lord Flowers as the "head" of the CVCP (p.109). In addition some minor errors have been noted, eg the statement that polytechnics can only award degrees for courses which have received CNAA recognition, whereas universities can, and do, award degrees for polytechnic courses that they validate (p.3), and omission of reference to the access by HMI to University Department of Education (p.18). A more serious reservation is the treatment of "tenure" for universities. On p.99 the assertion is made that university lecturers enjoy tenure. On p.105 this is qualified by "some" and on p.106 developed to employment until 67. It would have been better to have adopted a more cautious approach, emphasising that each university will have at least one form of contract, and many more than one: and that until each form of contract is tested in the courts the nature, significance and application of tenure remains a matter for speculation.

The author, in his evaluation, detects, in common with all those involved in education, an increase in conflict within the system, and attributes this partly to domestic factors: the impact of enforced economies, organisational changes, the challenge of the new technology (though this is very much a lightweight theme compared with the others) and the ending of the educational partnership; and partly to legal factors: the legal rights "industry", improved rights enforcement prospects, uncertainties in the legislation, the European dimension; together with the wider social influences on education law, the multi-racial society, and population changes. Many of the themes, however, receive scant treatment in the body of the book.

This epitomises some of the reservations about the book. It tries to cover too much ground in the space available, and it would have been better if some section had been omitted: post-compulsory education, or education as an arena in which a different conflict is taking place eg. Equal Opportunities and Race Relations. In a book entitled *Educational* conflict the main topic should have been conflict over *Educational* issues, with discussion of conflict over resource and other regulatory questions taking second place. The study is interesting, but the opportunity it presented has not been exploited to best advantage.

F. T. Mattison
Registrar
University of Hull

Teacher Careers: Crises and Continuities
By Patricia Sikes, Lynda Measor and Peter Woods
Falmer Press (London) 1985
pp. VI + 263

This is a very carefully planned volume, attractively presented and with an excellent introduction. The life-span of a teacher is looked at from the personal viewpoint of individual classroom teachers at different stages of their careers.

The teachers who have contributed are specialists in Art and Design and Sciences. Both men and women teachers are involved in the survey. To complete the diversification of the research the teachers were chosen from a Conservative controlled authority in the south of England and a Labour controlled authority in the North. From the outset the authors have set themselves a formidable task of collating so many subjective views from widely differing backgrounds. This is only part of the difficulty involved in canvassing subjective, and hence sincerely held, convictions but, as acknowledged in the Introduction, "many interests are shared among groups of teachers". Views from the different age-groups are felt to be necessary for this study of a full life-span of teaching.

The survey is broadened by looking at the teacher's life out of school. Inevitably shortcomings of administrators and inadequate funding also have their place in this survey.

These ends are neatly drawn together on page 2 where the "adult career" of a teacher is described as the product of a "dialectical relationship between self and circumstances". The task of producing a coherent unit of survey from such a wide range of topics and sources, in 250 pages, seems a daunting one. The amount of space given to transcriptions of tapes leaves less than enough room for the authors' comments, and there is a contrast in styles of expression which makes it difficult to read the book through with any feeling of continuity (p.32 "It was unprofessional conduct *to belt a kid*" and p.35 "a therapeutically cathartic experience".)

The effects of ageing on teachers is given much space without making any startling revelations. "Teachers are first and foremost people" is not a statement likely to raise serious questions but most will admit that class teaching is a role to be played wearing the appropriate mask. It is in acting out this role that many teachers overcome the tedium of routine and introduce the elements of fun and enjoyment which helps teacher and pupils to survive. Nobody in this book has much to say about enjoyment, and it seems a pity that there is so much of querulous cynicism in so many teachers' comments.

On management the authors recommend (p.154) a "participative organic structure". Training in management of personnel and resources would seem to be a firm prerequisite for the achievement of such an ideal, and few teachers have had such training. It is extremely difficult for anyone, inside or outside school, to assess a classroom teacher's natural gifts for management because once outside the classroom the rules of the game are changed completely. Traditions which have to evolve are not always in tune with changing times and, especially in the large comprehensive unit which may also provide community services, are no substitute for professional managerial competence based on training and experience.

The chapter on pupils influence reminds the reader that pupils, or "kids", as teachers insist on calling them, believe that teachers are there to impart information that will enable candidates to pass examinations. The difficulty of doing this in "mixed ability" is seen to put a heavy strain on the class teachers organisational and pedagogic skills. The situation is especially felt by teachers who depend on "subject knowledge" rather than "charisma" for their individual self-esteem.

A great number of tough, practical issues are raised in this 'slim volume'. The material is arranged with great skill and garnished throughout with a sprinkle of raw realistic comment from the Staff-room. There is plain evidence of total commitment to the teaching profession and an awareness of pupils' needs. With greater understanding, and adequate, funding, the teacher's career would be happier and more effective.

One feels that many of the difficulties could be met, at least in part, by increased opportunities for sabbatical leave to seek new information, experiment with new technology and generally take a short break from teaching to see what the rest of the education world is doing.

The formidable list of nearly two hundred authors quoted in this survey is a fair indication of the amount of time and energy a teacher needs to keep up-to-date with current thinking and research.

John Flynn
Institute of Education
University of Hull

Racism, Diversity and Education
Edited by Jagdish Gundara, Crispin Jones and Keith Kimberley. Pp.192.
London: Hodder and Stoughton (Studies in Teaching and Learning series), 1986. £4.95.

There is a logic to the structure of this book that is both refreshing and powerfully convincing: it moves from an excellent introduction by Gundara (which places these essays in context and which examines the terms of the field) through the historical background and the political dimension to the problems facing teachers and students in the classroom. It examines curriculum in the light of the theory and in view of developments over the last few years, and ends with an essay by Gillian Klein on the central role the library has to play in the establishing of a multicultural resource-based curriculum.

What struck me early in my reading of the book was the interesting difference in approach between this, with its focus clearly on combatting racism, and that of the 'multiculturalists'. There is the potential for a serious splitting of the ranks here, with those in the political front-line losing touch with – to mirror the over-simplification – the liberal theorists. I have yet to come across a book in this "field which manages to combine the forces, and yet combine they must if they are to make any real theoretical and practical advances.

Throughout, definition of terms is crucial. In particular, 'multicultural', 'multiethnic', 'multiracial' (with their obvious emphases on the diverse), 'black' and 'racism' itself all come under the microscope, and most usefully too. Much of the misunderstanding and lack of concerted progress in this area can be traced back to a muddling of the terms and a confusion about what, exactly, is being addressed. 'Black', as Peter Fraser points out, has undergone variations in emphasis during the last twenty years, and is used here in its inclusive sense. But the uncertainty over the term itself reflects accurately the basic issues at stake: the notion of equality and the "resolution of issues of diversity and uniformity with the nation state" (Gundara). That is why this book, unlike its 'multicultural' partners, sees sexism and classism as related evils.

Perhaps the best essay is that by Keith Kimberley, who charts recent developments in schools and looks at responses from the DES, LEAs and examining boards to the current climate of 'education for all'. He links such developments to the need for mixed-ability approaches, and faces squarely the fact that a "dynamic curriculum" – one which is flexible enough to reflect the perceived needs of the society – will be one that does not suppress uncomfortable contradictions. Interestingly, he cites the London Board's inclusion of Afro-Caribbean texts as a special option on the A-level English syllabus as typical of a well-intentioned move that only partially satisfies a need: he would like (and I agree with him here) to see those texts more fully integrated into the syllabus. But Kimberley's essay, and the book as a whole, does not take account of the widening of the net that is being offered to teachers by the GCSE criteria and syllabi.

It is this railing after the event that gives the book a somewhat dated feel. Developments are taking place quickly in this area, and although it is good to read a book which argues strongly and well for curriculum changes to reflect the diversity of our culture, there is the sense that improvements are being made at grass roots level without the full recognition of the contributors, locked as they seem to be in their dialectic.

Nevertheless, this is well worth reading. I would recommend the first few chapters then an à la carte approach, with Klein's essay (with its exposé of the racism enshrined in the Dewey classification system) to finish. A useful bibliography complements the text.

Richard Andrews
Lecturer in Education
University of Hull